Freud and Psychoanalysis

RICHARD STEVENS

Freud and Psychoanalysis

An Exposition and Appraisal

Open University Press

Milton Keynes : Philadelphia

Open University Press
12 Cofferidge Close
Stony Stratford
Milton Keynes MK11 1BY, England
and
1900 Frost Road, Suite 101
Bristol, PA 19007, USA

First Published 1983
Reprinted 1985, 1989

British Library Cataloguing in Publication Data

Stevens, Richard
    Freud, and psychoanalysis.
    1. Freud, Sigmund
    I. Title
    150.19′52   BF173.F85

    ISBN 0-335-10801-1

Printed in Great Britain by St Edmundsbury Press Limited
Bury St Edmunds, Suffolk

CONTENTS

Conclusion

PREFACE

This book is about the psychoanalytic way of making sense of personality, in particular as seen through the work of Freud. The purpose of Part One is to present his ideas clearly and succinctly and yet in a way which reflects their development and complexity.

The aim of Part Two is not only to assess his contribution but to examine what kind of understanding psychoanalysis offers. While research on its propositions is comprehensively reviewed here, it is argued that a more important task is to explore its implications. What does psychoanalysis lead us to conclude about the nature of mental life? What does it have to suggest about the ways in which we might lead our lives? What kind of understanding can we expect any theory of personality to provide?

An aspect of psychoanalysis which is emphasized is its potential in helping us to make sense of the conflicts and integrations which are an inevitable part of the experience of living. As a way of introducing psychoanalysis and briefly setting it in the context of other approaches to the study of personality, the source of contradictions within the self and the problems which arise from their resolution are discussed in the opening chapter.

While the book will be of particular interest to psychology students, it is a topic which has relevance to us all. Anyone interested, as layman or professional, in why people behave and feel as they do, is likely to find something of value in the ideas presented here. For they provoke thought about how we can understand both others and ourselves.

PERSONAL ACKNOWLEDGEMENTS

I would like to thank Derek Forrest, Judith Greene and Marie Jahoda for their encouragement, Jane Henry for her comments and John Skelton, my editor, for his patience and measured advice. All along the way there has been the invaluable secretarial assistance of Ortenz Opheelia Rose and the support and perspicacity of Margaret, my wife. My thanks too to Pat Vasiliou for her help with the typing, and to Bill Pickup for his understanding and efficiency.

INTRODUCTION

CHAPTER 1

The Individual as Integrator

The Multiple Self

Integration is a central process in our apprehension of the world. I look out from my high window; red brick, red-roofed houses, a tracery of trees beyond. I look more closely. Buff curtains flutter at a half-open window. On a gable end a clay gargoyle perches, wings outstretched; long black drainpipe with a square bucket top; innumerable serried lines of symmetrical tiles, a dark patch where two have slipped; green leaves touched with the rust of coming autumn. I could search for hours and still not exhaust the details that confront my eyes. But when I *glance* out, what I see is two houses with trees behind. I somehow select from the mass of detail and integrate it into a meaningful whole.

Selection and integration are features too of the way we lead our lives. Think for a moment of the vast array of things you could do tomorrow: take a train journey to any of a thousand destinations; speak to people you have never seen before; eat food you have not yet tasted; move, behave, dress, interact as you have never done before. Even if you are bed-ridden, there are innumerable different books and magazines to read, games to play, songs to sing. You can meditate, shout, write a letter to a friend or telephone a stranger. But many of these things you would never do. They are just not 'you'. They have no place in the pattern of your life. We select from the myriad courses of action open to us. We structure and integrate them into a coherent and characteristic style of life. A style of life which, partly at least, reflects as well as creates who we are – our self or identity.

Sometimes, we are aware of conflict between alternatives. A child in bed in the small hours of Christmas morning may feel the heavy parcels on the bottom of the bed, want to open them there and then and yet hesitate – it is not yet quite the prescribed time. Both courses of action are desirable. They are both within the spectrum of things that express his 'self'. They are both, if you like, integrations of which he as a person is capable. And yet only one is possible. Such moments of conflict arise for most of us every day. We (or 'part of us') want to do one thing, we also (or 'another part of us') want to do something else. Saturday can be spent fishing or painting the house. We can blow our top at a colleague's behaviour or grin and bear it. Many such conflicts are fairly easily resolved. We paint the house this week and go fishing the next. Others are more insidious in their consequences. Whatever choice we make, the conflict remains with us.

A week ago, a new member joined a group I run. The others welcomed Mike and tried to make him feel at home but it was obvious that he was ill at ease. In conversation he was often aggressive, in activities unco-operative. Last night, he opened up. He told us of the conflict he had experienced that first evening. He wanted to come to the group. He longed to be with and get close to others and yet, at the same time, he dreaded facing so many new people. Conflict. Two mutually incompatible drives within him – to make contact, to avoid contact. To satisfy one would be to frustrate the other. Mike's means of resolving the conflict, he told us, had been beer. Before coming on that first evening, he had gone to a pub and drunk for an hour. The effects of the alcohol had sufficiently blunted his apprehension to enable him to come along. This had resolved the conflict as far as action was concerned but the emotional turbulence within him had been only partly stilled. Underlying conflict still remained. The group noticed its expression in the negative, aggressive style of his behaviour.

There are two features worth noting in this illustration. First, it suggests that actions may have multiple meaning. Mike's behaviour was an expression of both his desire to come and his anxiety about doing so. Secondly, motivations which are denied direct outlet may nevertheless find indirect means of expression. Mike's suppressed anxiety about meeting people had made his behaviour when he came to the group so antagonistic that it might well have led people to avoid contact with him, thus indirectly fulfilling its aim.

It is perhaps only too easy to think of a person as a *unity*, to assume that he either likes or dislikes, either desires or wants to avoid. After all, each of us behaves as one organism, bounded by one body and tending to experience and to do one thing at a time. But outward unity masks inward complexity. Within us, different forces and desires pull in oblique or contrary directions. Actions often have multiple meaning, express multiple motivations. Such complexity and conflict may underlie not only behaviour but also the ways in which we experience the world about us. Consider, for example, emotional reactions to people. Think of a few people you know well – not necessarily close friends. Sift carefully your feelings about them. You may be aware of *ambivalence*. On one level you are attracted by them or you admire them, on another they are less appealing, perhaps even repellent to you. Such ambivalence may be a result of the fact that a person is a complex stimulus. Each individual presents a host of attitudes, behaviours, characteristics to which you can react. Or equally, it may result from the different strands that interweave to form your self, so that while one part of you may be rather amused by an action, another is a little shocked by it.

Why is it that individuals are characterized by such inner complexity and conflict?

Evolutionary Origins of Complexity

People are the outcome of evolution on a time-scale which, although we can label it with numbers, eludes our effective comprehension. Low down on the evolutionary scale, an organism's behaviour is controlled by genetically programmed tendencies in interaction with environmental contingencies. Higher up the scale the programming becomes looser and learning begins to play a progressively greater role. But the critical feature which distinguishes man is the evolution of physiological structures which make language possible. This enormously increases both the power to communicate and to conceptualize experience of natural and social worlds as well as the inner world of thoughts and feelings. The transmission of beliefs and customs through culture and relationships powerfully supplement biology and direct learning from experience as the primary shapers of actions and awareness. Our lives become steered by the symbolic – by knowledge outside the range of direct experience, by ideals and values quite unrelated to the natural world – or even, like Don Quixote, become stimulated by fantasy. The symbolic is real enough both in our experience and in the tangible effects of our own and other people's actions (a person may build a church or even kill for his beliefs), but our evolutionary past remains with us – we are still biological creatures in a physical world. It is the very power and richness of our symbolic capacity which, while so far helping us to survive, also makes inner conflict more likely and the task of integration so problematic.

A person's experience of self in relation to the world might be considered then to have three kinds of aspect or source. Man is an organism governed by biological processes and physiological needs. At the same time, his capacity for symbolic thinking enables him to 'internalize' the external world. He becomes aware of the nature of reality and the constraints which it imposes on him in his attempts to gratify his needs.

Thirdly, man is capable of 'internalizing' not only the physical world about him but aspects of the social context in which he lives. He assimilates many of the perceived characteristics, values, feelings, ideas and ways of conceptualizing of those people who are close to him. His emotional reactions may be influenced by the nature of his relationships with them and by the conceptions they have sown of the kind of person he is or should be.

The desires and constraints which stem from these three sources are often difficult to reconcile with each other and this may create conflict within a person. For example, body processes may urge against actions which awareness of the reality of a situation prescribes as necessary for maximum gratification or even for survival. A lost and weary climber may long to lie down and rest in the snow but reality perception knows that to give way to such an urge would spell death. Biological and reality processes may work together and be in conflict with those aspects of self which derive from assimilation of cultural concepts and ideals. So Scott sought the South Pole because of the achievement success would bring, in spite of the torturous bodily effort his journey involved and even though he knew that death shadowed him and, indeed, finally caught him and his companions there. These are but dramatic examples of the conflicts operative within us most of the time. Possibly, at this moment, you are suppressing sleepiness or the need for a cup of coffee in order to carry on reading this book. Perhaps yesterday you resisted temptation. You wanted to do something but you didn't because you thought it would be wrong or you might get caught, get your fingers burned, risk a marriage, lose your job or put on weight.

These three aspects of self should not be seen as clearly separate and distinct. Biological and internalized 'reality' and 'social' process interlock together as length, breadth and depth combine to yield volume. Each can only be viewed properly in relation to the others. There may be conflict too between desires and constraints arising from the same kind of source. One physiological need may vie with another, one ideal with another, or two courses of action may appear equally profitable. It is probably the case though, as we shall see later, that such conflicts are not usually as significant in their consequences as those between forces emanating from different sources.

The Child Within

Time is woven inevitably into the fabric of all human enterprise. To appreciate more fully the sources of inner complexity, we need to look at a person not just in terms of our evolution as a species (phylogenesis) but also in the context of a particular individual's development (ontogenesis) and his view of the possible personal futures which lie ahead.

One notable feature of the human species is the very long period of development preceding adulthood. Underlying the functioning of every adult is a complex personal history. As Piaget has demonstrated, a child should not be considered merely as a miniature, less-developed version of an adult. A child is *qualitatively* different. It seems likely, too, that the conflicts experienced by children are of a qualitatively different kind from those of normal adults. For one reason, the three processes we have assumed to be significant in generating inner conflict operate differently at different stages of the child's development. Take the perception of reality as one example. Piaget has shown that the child does not properly understand conservation until the age of about six onwards. Pour liquid from a broad into a narrower container, for example, and before this age, he is likely to assume that, because the level has risen, there is now more, even though nothing has been added or taken away. Not until about six does he really grasp the idea of causality. The young child lives in a world in which fantasy is not clearly distinguished from reality, in which actions are presumed to influence events in ways which to the adult would appear quite illogical or magical. Significant features of a child's world – a toy, part of the body, a picture in a book – may assume disproportionate prominence. Fears may be exaggerated and unrealistic. The child may also fantastically overestimate the potential power of his own actions. Thus, the reality to which the child accommodates must be very different from that of the adult. Conflicts generated are quite probably more intense and overwhelming. It would seem reasonable to suppose that infantile fears and expectations are more prone to exaggeration and distortion, unconstrained as they are by the same bounds of logic, order and causality that characterize the more stable, waking world of the normal adult.

How likely is it that experiences of such magnitude would merely fade away? They form a vivid part of the child's experience. More probably, like other aspects of his physical and social worlds, they are internalized and become part of the person he is, remaining with him, albeit transformed, in later life. So adult anxieties may cloak a residue of infantile fears. A child is father to every man: the conflicts of an adult may echo the emotional memories and conflicts of the child he once was. Studying or retracing the conflicts experienced by the developing child may well provide interesting insights into adult integrations.

Growing up is not just a process of progressive acquisition and expression of skills and characteristics. From childhood to old age inner conflicts confront us. From a very early age, the child plays very much an active role in his own development. But parents and others around him impose constraints on his spontaneous expression and actions and required him to develop self direction and control. So the child comes to express emotions, for example, in a form expected in his culture. The little boy learns perhaps to check his tears – it's not brave to cry. By adolescence, the expression of sorrow may no longer be weeping but merely a lump in the throat; the expression of anger no longer shouting and stamping in rage but a quiet clenching of the fists. Such shaping may be so profound that even when an adult desires to weep, he may find he cannot do so. Slowly the child learns, too, to curb his impulse for direct gratification. He learns that under certain circumstances punishment or pain may ensue, or that the greater reward possible by postponement makes it pay to wait. He learns to modify his desires in obedience to the wishes of others – either because they control the situation or because of the guilt he experiences as a result of his internalization of their values and prohibitions.

Gradually, the child evolves a concept of self – of who and what he is – shadowy at first but increasing in clarity the older he grows. In part, this self concept will be based on direct experience of himself – what he likes, dislikes, can do and cannot do. In part, also, it will be based on others' reactions to him, on what they seem to think he is. Much of his self concept will depend on his assimilation of their imposed values and definitions. She's a 'naughty child' so her *self* should feel guilty. 'He's not a very bright boy' so his *self* shrinks in the face of competition. As we grow into adolescence and adulthood, so the roles we assume also impose their definitions upon us. The soldier at war 'hates his enemy'. The mother 'loves her child at all times'. The tutor 'cares about the academic progress of her student'. But what if they don't? The soldier may know very well that the man he is shooting at is just like himself. Love may be the last emotion experienced by the mother faced with her screaming, demanding baby. Research or even tending her roses may be of more absorbing interest to the tutor than the progress of her pupil.

Throughout life we have to learn to cope with constraints imposed by ourselves and others and with the conflicts created by internalization of physical and social worlds. We develop means of coping with anxiety and threat, means of resolving conflicts. We can deny or repress, for example, a feeling or desire which conflicts with another aspect of ourselves. Or, alternatively, we can act it out. Or we can impute intentions and characteristics to ourselves and/or to others in order to maintain consistency with a desired image of self. The ways in which we resolve inner conflict, like the nature of the conflicts themselves, are likely to change as we develop. A child's world is more fluid and *autistic* than that of an adult, i.e., it is more determined by wishes and fantasies and less constrained by considerations of causality, time and space. It is therefore far easier for him to deny aspects of reality and seek recourse to fantasy solutions than it is for the normal adult, at least as far as an adult's conscious functioning is concerned.

A person's identity emerges from the continuous and changing interplay over time between biological predispositions and assimilations like these from environmental and social contexts. It will be a function of the characteristic ways in which these varied aspects are integrated and internal conflicts resolved. Underlying any individual action lies this complex configuration of identity. Not surprisingly, actions often have multiple meanings not necessarily immediately apparent in their overt form.

Unconscious and Conscious Conflict

Many of the conflicts illustrated or implied in the preceding discussion have been unconscious. The use of repression or denial to resolve conflict merely banishes it from awareness. A mother may deny feelings of hositility towards her child because they are not in keeping with her concept of herself as a good mother. But like Mike's suppressed apprehension, the emotional force of this conflict is not necessarily dispelled by such a resolution. It may take the form of unreasoned anxiety. Or the hostility may express itself indirectly; thus Mike's antagonistic behaviour may well have reflected his suppressed desire to avoid contact. So perhaps this mother may 'accidentally' be late with a feed or prick the baby's skin while pinning a nappy. Alternatively, she may resolve the conflict by seeing her child as naughty and therefore feel justified in smacking or shouting at him. In rare cases, she could even momentarily forget her *self* and the kind of person she thinks herself to be and act out her repressed hostility in direct attack. As we shall see later, the residues of infantile fears and conflicts underlying the anxieties of the adult are often operative at an unconscious level. It was the particular contribution of Freud to show us the significance of unconscious conflict and to begin to unravel the way it works.

Other conflicts which a person confronts are conscious. The development of the complex capacity for symbolic thought and language which is such a significant human characteristic and which exacerbates rather than reduces the burden of conflict, generates existential problems. For a person can conceptualize not only the world about him but also himself and the shadow of his future. Although he desires to live, he knows that he will die. He knows that his own actions help determine the future to come. Man is perhaps unique in that he can regret or be proud of what he has done and envisage himself as other than he is. Thus an individual may find him or herself with a further task of integration – subjective choice from the array of possible actions and identities he can conceive. Which of the possibilities that confront him should he take up? It has been later psychoanalysts like Erikson and Fromm whose work has extended to consider issues like these.

Such explicit problems of conflict and integration are particularly characteristic of adolescence. Individual development and culture conspire to confront the adolescent with critical choices. What occupation should he choose? What life-style, values, way of relating to others? The child's world is too constrained, he is not yet stabilized enough, nor is he likely to have yet developed the cognitive capacity for such conscious choice to become a problem. Most adults have made their choice and have embedded themselves in roles and contexts where choice of identity is no longer such an open possibility. Erikson[1] argues that creative people are particularly prone to extend the period of identity diffusion, perhaps because their imagination poses too rich an array of possibilities for them to resolve easily and integrate their lives into a set and coherent pattern. Identity diffusion is uncomfortable. It is less confusing and stressful to come down on one side or the other and to develop a consistency in the fabric of one's life. On the other hand, identity choice involves the rejection of other possible identities or potential aspects of our lives – what William James has called our 'abandoned' or 'murdered' selves. We respond according to our 'majority self', the identity which we have come to assume. In an interesting novel, *The Diceman*, the American writer, Luke Rhinehart[2] explores the problem of giving expression to 'abandoned' selves. The method adopted by the New York psychiatrist who is the main character in the book, is to introduce into his life, control not by self but by chance. At decision points in his life, he sets up the options open to him, including some which 'he' would never normally do, and determines his action by a throw of the dice. Many adults make less stylized attempts to break out of a too encapsulating identity at some point in their lives; by taking up a new job, residence, life-style or by trying consciously to change the way they feel and react.

Conscious and unconscious conflicts are not to be thought of as clearly separable. We may be aware of existential conflicts only in the anxiety they arouse and their influence on our behaviour. And the particular dilemmas which exercise consciousness may well be rooted in unconscious needs or forgotten episodes from a childhood past.

The Study of Personality

The area of psychology concerned with the study of the whole person and why we behave and experience in the way that we do is personality theory. This comes in many forms originating from different traditions within psychology. It is not the purpose of this book to review these. Nevertheless, indicating something of their diversity and nature may help to make clear why psychoanalysis and the ideas of Freud are particularly relevant to our understanding of the kinds of process indicated above.

Psychoanalysis has been the most influential perspective in the study of personality. Theories in this tradition have emerged essentially from the clinical work of the theorists as therapists, from their own self-analysis and from the general awareness of the human condition they have gleaned from their study of philosophy, science and the arts.

Academic psychologists, uncomfortable with psychoanalysts' emphasis on interpretation, have attempted to apply, in contrast, tradition scientific procedures of measurement and experiment in research on personality. 'Trait' or factor theories[3] are usually based on statistical analyses of questionnaire responses, observations of behaviour and personal life, data like age, whether married etc., in order to see which items cluster together. Personality is conceptualized as a profile of a person's rating on factors or dimensions (like introversion/extraversion, anxiety, excitability etc.) which have been elicited in this fashion. The insistence of some factor theorists like Eysenck that personality has an inherited, biological basis, sets them off from learning theorists who focus exclusively on the significance of environmental events in the reinforcing and shaping of behaviours. But both believe that progress in psychology will come only with the use of measurement and experiments.

Personality theorists who adopt what we might loosely term a phenomenological–existential–humanistic perspective take issue with psychoanalysis on a rather different point – what they see as an over-emphasis by orthodox psychoanalysis on unconscious motivation. Their phenomenological approach takes an individual's conscious awareness as the focal point of interest. The way a person makes sense of the world is regarded as underpinning what he does and also as a source of interest in its own right. Existential issues like self-awareness and choice are seen as central. Most theorists of this type could probably be considered humanistic in that they believe in the capacity of a person for self-directed change and growth. Such theorists come from diverse backgrounds. Some, like Ludwig Binswanger and Ronald Laing, have been psychiatrists who developed their ideas as alternatives to more orthodox treatments. Others, like Maslow, Rogers and Kelly, have come from academic psychology. As befits their background, the latter tend to place greater emphasis on formal research. This third tradition has close links with psychoanalysis. Their method is very often interpretative. Many of the theorists have been psychoanalysed or acknowledge the influence of psychoanalysis on their ideas and more recent theorizing in psycho-analysis has tended to move towards their position by placing greater emphasis on conscious experience.

The experience of changing perspective from one theory to another is often like travelling to a distant country, so different are their concepts and concerns. Even the methods they use for investigating and verifying may be totally unalike. That there should be such variability among personality theories is a fascinating issue in its own right. The key point to appreciate is that these theories (like any other theory or form of knowledge) are not to be regarded as mere reflections of some 'reality out there'. We cannot simply go out and check which theory or hypothesis is best by testing them against reality. For a start, the questions they ask may not be anything like the same. And, even if we can find a common issue on which they are at odds, there may not be agreement as to the form a test should take or what kind of evidence would constitute support.

What a theorist chooses to investigate and how he investigates and conceptualizes it, will depend on the assumptions he makes, albeit implicitly, about the nature of psychology and of people. His theories will be constructions or creations which reflect his interests, charac-teristics and background as well as the phenomena he is investigating.[4]

Recent psychobiographical studies of selected theorists have begun to unravel some of the links between aspects of a theory and the personality of the theorist and events in his life.[5] While psychoanalytic theorists naturally lend themselves as subjects for such examination because of their extensive use of self-analysis as a source of ideas, more self-avowedly scientific theorists like Skinner have also been examined in this way.[6] Theories of this kind are just as much constructions. They depend, for example, on the ungrounded (and often unquestioned) epistemological assumption that psychological phenomena can be effec-tively measured and that it is appropriate to extend to psychology the methods of traditional science such as experiments and search for general laws.

The notion of theories as constructions should not be taken to imply a position of *relativism* – that any one theory is necessarily as good as any other and you just take your choice according to your fancy. For theories are the outcome of an *interaction* between the theorist and the phenomena being studied. His theory determines what he looks at and how, but in turn it is likely to be influenced by what he finds. As the sociologist Israel has put it: 'The relationship between theory and reality is *mutual*. Theories organize data; theories confer meaning upon them. Neverthe-less data cannot be arbitrarily organized: theories have to take into account the "structure of reality".[7] The constructional position essentially implies *relativity* i.e., that a theory can be judged only from a standpoint which itself depends on a set of assumptions and a way of construing reality. There is no *objective* standpoint from which they can all be compared. It does mean that the value placed on any particular theory will be a function of the needs and characteristics of the evaluator and of the use to which the theory is to be put. It also emphasizes that any personality theory carries with it certain assumptions about what a person is like.

The model of the person which emerges from the earlier discussion of the individual as integrator involves the following assumptions.

1. It is *holistic*, i.e., it emphasizes the need to look at the whole person, that each aspect takes on meaning only in relation to the whole. If you want to understand why an individual acts and feels as he does, it is no use just looking at factors such as environment, constitution or intellectual capacity in isolation.
2. It is a *dynamic* conception. Actions and feelings are conceived of as the outcome of the interplay of forces (dynamics) of different kinds.
3. Actions and experiences may have underlying and *multiple meaning* other than that which they may appear overtly to represent. They may be influenced by motivations of which the individual is unaware.
4. It adopts a *developmental perspective*. Childhood experiences and conflicts are assumed to be potentially of considerable significance for the characteristics and behaviour of an adult.
5. There is a concern with *inner conflict and integration* and the particular configuration of conflict resolutions, values and characteristic modes of emotional response which underlie an individual's actions and experience.

By no means do all theories of personality fit in with such assumptions. Not all are dynamic, for example, or emphasize the significance of conflict and integration. Trait theories, as we have seen, conceptualize personality in a rather more static way as a collection of traits. Behaviourist approaches generally, with their emphases on measurement and experiment, eschew meaning as subject-matter, at least in so far as this involves interpretation. And although phenomenological psychologists do put meaning at the centre of the stage, their concern is less with unconscious and multiple levels of meaning than with its conscious representation. They also tend to focus more on the 'here and now' situation of a person than on his developmental past.

The approach which best fits the model of the person outlined above is psychoanalysis. Freudian theory contains the fundamentals of the psychoanalytic approach and this is the subject of Part One. After an account of Freud's life, the subsequent chapters each deal with a central aspect of Freud's theory including his explanation of neuroses and his method of therapy. This presentation of the fundamentals of psycho-analysis concludes with a review of the main lines of development in psychoanalytic thought since Freud's original formulations.

Part Two then explores what kind of understanding is offered by psychoanalysis. What sort of theory is it? It is argued that it has two key features: an *integrative* capacity to take into account and interrelate the wide range of factors which underlie any individual personality, and the *hermeneutic* power to help us interpret the meanings of actions and experience. But how valid are the interpretations it offers? Research studies which bear on the propositions of psychoanalysis are extensively reviewed. The key question which emerges is how far are such assess-ments appropriate given the nature of the subject matter with which psychoanalysis is concerned? The confusion which seems endemic to discussions of the issue arises, it will be asserted, because of the double roots of mental life in both biology and symbolic experience. Part Two concludes by discussing some of the implications of psychoanalysis both for society and the way we lead our lives.

The notion of theories as constructions will be elucidated by relating the background and characteristics of Freud the man to his work. Epi-stemological issues will also be taken up. One of the difficulties in the way of finding an effective means of conceptualizing conflict and inte-gration is the simultaneous complexity involved. Many processes are assumed to be operative at the same time. Such multi-dimensionality is not easy to capture in the linear focus of words and propositions. The psychoanalytic approach essentially involves feeling for pattern, con-figuration. It stresses differentiation – giving meaning and sense to phenomena, seeing the ways in which its different aspects interrelate – rather than formulating a set of rigorously testable propositions. Thus, as will be discussed later, laboratory testing is usually neither appropriate nor effectively possible to apply. This raises the question as to how far the methods of traditional natural science, which have been taken by most academic psychologists to be the *sine qua non* of an effective psychology, are appropriate. Might not a dialectical approach which took full account of the constructional nature of knowledge, sought explanation in the interplay of forces rather than causal relationships, and which acknowledged the significance of pattern, meaning and taking a developmental perspective, serve psychology better? This issue is introduced in Part Two but addressed more directly in the final chapter of the book.

Psychoanalytic concepts have been derived not from experiment or even from structured observation but from self-analysis and the intimate study of patients in psychotherapy. One way of evaluating the theory (and also much of the discussion earlier in this section) is in terms of how effectively it makes sense of the phenomena in question and of your own experience. Try to bear this in mind as you read. In an appendix there are also some suggestions for activities which may be of help, should you wish to try them, in the process of exploring your own self.

Part One

FREUD AND PSYCHOANALYSIS

Psychoanalysis is the creation of Sigmund Freud. He originated its major methods, ideas and concepts. Although many new concepts and variations have been put forward by other psychoanalysts, the essence of the psychoanalytic perspective is contained in Freud's work.

It is not really possible to give an account of Freudian theory which is brief and, at the same time, conveys effectively the authentic flavour of the psychoanalytic approach. Indeed, such an attempt can be positively misleading for Freud's theory does not form a coherent, unified and monolithic system. His ideas evolved and changed during the course of his lifetime. Like any other theory, psychoanalysis is a construction – a conceptualization designed to make sense of the varied phenomena of behaviour and experience. Freud himself described his theory as a 'mythology'. His use of animistic imagery to conceptualize intangible mental phenomena invites misunderstanding when it is set out in the confines of a brief account. Both as theory and therapeutic method, psychoanalysis is essentially a quest for meaning. It began as an attempt to make sense of the subtleties, paradoxes, banalities and obscurities of behaviour and experience, the turmoil and convolutions of emotion which Freud encountered both in his work as a psychotherapist and in his own introspections. Perhaps primarily Freud was a philosopher, literally a lover of wisdom or knowledge. He sought to understand his subject matter – the human life within and around him. When he began, although there were many clues left by earlier writers, philosophers and psychologists, there were few tools and techniques of use to him, either as a therapist or as a seeker after understanding. Freud's task was to develop new methods for exposing the delicate fabric of behaviour and experience and to try to fit together in some pattern the pieces which emerged. It is as a tool for making sense of the providing insights into the phenomena of mental life that psychoanalysis comes into its own. In the pages which follow, I have tried to sketch out those aspects of Freudian theory which are fundamental to any understanding of psychoanalysis, roughly following the chronological order in which Freud developed his ideas. There are three sets of ideas which form the mainspring of psycho-analytic theory: the *operation of the unconscious, psychosexual development*, and *psychodynamics* (the interplay of different forces within the individual and its consequences). To set these in context the chapters which consider them are preceded by a brief account of the course and nature of Freud's life.

CHAPTER 2

Freud — The Man

A 200 foot steeple was perhaps the only distinguishing characteristic of the little town of Freiberg, situated some 150 miles north-east of Vienna in what is now Czechoslovakia. It was here on the 6th of May in 1856 that Freud was born, the first child of the third wife of a cloth merchant. His father was 41 at the time of his birth and already had two grown-up sons from his first marriage. One of Freud's first playmates was his own nephew who was a year older than him. His mother, who was 20 years younger than her husband, eventually had seven more children but Sigmund remained her 'undisputed darling'. Freud has attributed his later self-confidence in the face of hostility to the fact that he was his mother's favourite. Although the family was Jewish, orthodox practices and beliefs were not emphasized. For a time, Sigmund had a Catholic nurse who would take him with her to mass.

In 1860 his father's business began to fail and the family moved, eventually settling in Vienna. At the Sperl Gymnasium there, Freud proved an able pupil, remaining top of his class for seven years. As an adolescent his interests were broad and varied. In addition to Latin and Greek, he could read both English and French fluently and had also taught himself Spanish and Italian. But it was towards literature and philosophy, towards human concerns, that his major interests lay. He considered law as a career, even politics, but such possibilities for a Viennese Jew of modest means were limited.

Pragmatically but somewhat reluctantly Freud decided on medicine and, at the age of 17 entered the University of Vienna. It was eight years before he graduated. After experimenting with chemistry and zoology (he carried out a laborious dissection study in search of the sex organs of male river eels), he settled to research in the physiology laboratory of Ernst Brücke where he remained for six years. There, he made a study of the spinal cord of a primitive form of fish, learning fine dissection and staining techniques and making his own drawings, and published numerous papers. Freud enjoyed research and it was only the insistent advice of his teacher that forced him to realize he had to earn a living. So he finally took his degree and, in 1882, entered the General Hospital in Vienna. As a junior physician, however, he was still able to carry on research and publishing, now in cerebal anatomy. Freud maintained an active interest in neurology until he was 41, later publishing monographs on both aphasia and cerebral palsy in children.

At the age of 29, with support from Brücke, he was appointed Lecturer (*Privatdozent*) in Neuropathology and, in the face of stiff competition, awarded a travelling scholarship which enabled him to study for five months with Charcot in Paris. With characteristic shrewdness Freud gained access to Charcot's inner circle by offering to translate the great man's works into German. It was here that Freud first encountered the use of hypnotic suggestion by which Charcot could induce or remove at will paralyses and anaesthesiae in certain patients. Freud was very impressed by Charcot and his stay in Paris marked the beginning of his concern with the psychological as opposed to the physiological basis of neurosis.

Since childhood days Freud had been dominated by the desire to be famous. A popular family anecdote recounted how a peasant woman had prophesied that he would be a great man. While still in his twenties, Freud was writing to his fiancée about his 'future biographers'. His initial ideal of the great hero (Hannibal had been his favourite) gradually became replaced by the ambition to be a great discoverer in science. He became excited by the potential of the drug cocaine, particularly its properties of reducing pain and creating lasting exhilaration. Freud found using the drug helped him overcome the periodic bouts of depression and apathy to which he was prone. With the possibility of using his investigations as a way to making a name for himself he wrote a paper on the drug and, not fully realizing its addictive properties, indiscriminately advocated its use to his family and friends. One of his closest friends Fleischl eventually developed a severe addiction which later in part contributed to his death.

In his personal life Freud appeared, at least on the surface, to be a model of Victorian propriety. Although his 900 letters to his fiancée Martha Bernays (they were apart three of the four and a half years they were engaged) show the passionate quality of his feelings, even here he felt it necessary, with the prudishness of the period, to apologize for even a casual allusion to her feet! As Ernest Jones, his friend and biographer put it: 'Freud was someone whose instincts were far more powerful than those of the average man but whose repressions were even more potent!'

Freud's letters[1] also reveal the breadth of his interests and cultural knowledge. They are full of detailed and perceptive references to literature and history, both Classical and European and to paintings and plays. He collected antiquities all his life and, in 1931, commented in a letter to a friend (Stefan Zweig) that he had 'read more archeology than psychology'. While at university, Freud had taken additional courses in philosophy and later was recommended by his old professor, Brentano, to translate into German some writings of the English philosopher J. S. Mill.

Immediately after his marriage at the age of 30, Freud started in private practice. On his return from Paris, he had given a presentation on Charcot's work to the Society of Medicine. This, he felt, had been received negatively and for the next six years he largely withdrew from scientific work and concentrated instead on his patients. The inadequacy of the methods currently in use for the treatment of 'nervous diseases' forced him to seek for new and more effective weapons for his 'therapeutic arsenal.' He discarded the then popular electrotherapy as having 'no more relation to reality than an Egyptian dream book.' In its place he used hypnosis (which he had seen used by Charcot and later by Bernheim at Nancy) to enable patients to recall forgotten events and for making suggestions to modify their subsequent behaviour. Even this method Freud found limited as it was not possible to hypnotize all his patients or to always produce a sufficient depth of trance for suggestion to be effective.

Josef Breuer, one of Freud's older and supportive friends, had developed a new technique for treating hysteria, a condition which results in paralyses and other physical disturbances arising without any apparent organic basis. Breuer had hypnotized Bertha Pappenheim, a talented, attractive young patient, had relaxed her and encouraged her to talk about anything that came into her head. Eventually the girl recounted in detail, and with full emotional reactions, a painful incident which she had repressed from awareness, and her symptoms disappeared. Freud reasoned that traumatic events, though forgotten, could still be operative at an unconscious level and were the direct cause of the physical symptoms of the hysteria. The collaboration of Freud and Breuer culminated in their joint publication in 1895 of *Studies in Hysteria*. A mutual attraction developed between Breuer and Bertha. When his wife became jealous, complaining that he could talk about no one else, Breuer broke off treatment, never to return to his 'cathartic' method, and took his wife to Venice for a second honeymoon. Freud, however, persevered. He refined the technique of free association which he gradually used to replace hypnosis. Through his experiences with patients and perhaps more importantly his own protracted self-analysis, he gradually came to focus attention on childhood and to place particular emphasis on the key role of early sexual development in the formation of neurosis.

His self-analysis reached its peak in 1897, the year after his father's death, and helped to generate the groundwork for much of his theory to come. Analysing his own dreams and checking background details with his mother, Freud confronted the residues of repressed emotions from his own childhood – destructive and ambivalent feelings towards his father, intense affection for his mother, guilt at the death of his infant brother Julius.

The year 1900 saw the publication of the first major work on psychoanalysis: *The Interpretation of Dreams*. In this Freud sets out his theory of the unconscious and of repression and attempts to show how mental phenomena such as dreams and neurosis are a product of conflict between different mental systems. The book was either ignored or reviewed badly and it took six years to sell the 600 copies printed (Freud received less than £50 from its publication). The *Three Essays on the Theory of Sexuality* came in 1905. In this, his second major publication on psychoanalysis, he formalizes his ideas on the development of the sexual instinct from infancy to maturity and demonstrates the intrinsic relationship between development in early childhood and sexual perversion and neurosis in the adult.

A band of devoted followers, later to become the Vienna Psychoanalytical Society, gradually began to gather round Freud. He was particularly gratified by the support and interest shown by Carl Jung, a young Swiss psychiatrist. By now Freud had been appointed to a professorship and, with the growing international recognition of psychoanalysis, he was invited in 1909 to Clark University in the USA to receive an honorary doctorate and to deliver a series of guest lectures. (Freud prepared these in his characteristic way during the course of a brisk half-hour walk immediately before each lecture.) Psychoanalysis began to grow into a flourishing movement. Congresses were held, a journal established and in 1910 the International Psychoanalytic Society was formed.

Freud now lived in the comfortable style of the Viennese middle-class. He had fathered six children and his household included his sister-in-law Minna, in whom he found a good and possibly intimate friend, as well as several servants. The pattern of his life was set and ordered. During both mornings and afternoons he would see his patients, the day being broken by an after-lunch stroll in nearby streets. The evening would usually be devoted to his scientific writings and correspondence. Freud remained an enthusiastic letter writer. It had been his correspondence with Wilhelm Fliess, a Berlin medical specialist and close friend, which had stimulated and sustained him during the years before his recognition. On Saturdays, Freud would relax in typical Viennese style with a game of cards. He spent holidays with his family in rented country houses and, with his younger brother, made several forays to the Mediterranean visiting Athens, Rome and Crete. This was, on the whole, a time of tranquility for Freud, contrasting with the mood of earlier periods when he would often swing between elation and tiredness and despair.

In the following years came a steady stream of publications on psycho-analytic technique and theory including studies based on literature and biography. Freud now numbered the eminent among his patients who included, for example, Gustav Mahler. But they were years also marked by growing dissension in the close-knit psychoanalytic circle, which culminated in the secession of Adler from the group in 1911 followed, to Freud's especial sorrow, by Jung in 1914.

The end of the First World War saw Freud living in defeated Vienna on a diet of thin vegetable soup and treating patients in an unheated con-sulting room dressed in overcoat and gloves. In 1920 he published the most controversial and least accepted of all his works, *Beyond the Pleasure Principle*, where he postulated *Thanatos*, the instinct within us all that strives for death. One can speculate about the effects which his personal circumstances and the background and violence of the war may have had on his thinking. His own sons were called up and one had gone missing for several weeks. As a therapist, Freud had encountered the problem of soldiers suffering from shell shock and 'war neurosis'. And, in January of the year in which the monograph was published, his daughter Sophie died of influenza.

In the 'twenties Freud's work largely centred on the development of ego psychology, in particular on the analysis of the characteristic ways in which the ego is able to defend itself from the anxiety aroused by the external world and by repressed instinctual drives. His daughter Anna, the only one of Freud's children to follow in his footsteps, was to elaborate these ideas subsequently.

1923 was marred by the first symptoms of the cancer of the jaw that eventually led to thirty-three operations and was to torment Freud until the end of his life. By now he was enjoying world fame. In 1924 he was offered $25,000 or 'anything he cared to name' by the *Chicago Tribune* to psychoanalyse two murderers who had caught the headlines in the USA. Sam Goldwyn also offered Freud $100,000 to work on a film of famous love scenes from history. Freud refused both offers.

Freud's final writings, as for example *Civilization and its Discontents*,[2] were devoted to an analysis of man's relationship with society and the societal origins of guilt.

Hitler came to power in 1933. Shortly after, Freud's writings along with those of Einstein and H. G. Wells were blazing in public bonfires. Freud's reported reaction was 'What progress we are making. In the Middle Ages they would have burned me, now they are content with burning my books'.[3] Freud was still in Austria when the Nazi invasion took place in 1938. His apartment was searched by the Gestapo and his daughter Anna taken away for questioning for several hours. Eventually, after representations on their behalf had been made by Mussolini among others, the Freud family was allowed to leave for London. As a child, Freud had often dreamed of moving to England to live with his older step-brothers. He died there, in Hampstead, on 23 September 1939.

   There are qualities which shine clearly throughout the span of Freud's life and work. These include his openness, curiosity and willingness to explore, his honesty in confronting what he found and the courage of his preparedness (given the times) to reveal in his writings the most intimate details of himself where this was necessary to illustrate his ideas. The picture of Freud which emerges though from this brief review of his life is of a complex personality which, in many ways, seems expressive of polarities or coexisting, opposite characteristics. From the outside, the pattern of Freud's life may seem narrow and ordered. He lived at home until he was 28. He spent most of the rest of his life in his apartment at 19 Berggasse in Vienna. But the conventionality of his outward life hides an inner world of thought, imagination and adventure of quite extraordinary richness. Freud's letters and writings give the impression that he thought and speculated about almost everything he came into contact with. In the people of Paris he sees the ghosts of the French Revolution. Standing before the bust of Elizabeth I in Westminster Abbey, he wonders how far she was the inspiration to Shakespeare for his Lady Macbeth.
   I have already mentioned the contrast between the passionate anguish sometimes glimpsed through the window of his letters, and his reserve and propriety. Relationships with women were important to Freud – with his mother, his daughter Anna and his sister-in-law Minna, as well as his wife. Until recently it had been assumed that Martha had been his only sexual partner and some of his correspondence carries hints that this side of his marriage exhausted itself after relatively few years. (There is now some speculation that he may have had a secret affair in his forties with his wife's unmarried sister Minna. She had come to live with them and help with the family. Freud was certainly close to her and they went on several holidays alone together. Freud's then close colleague Jung dropped several hints in an interview just before his death that this relationship had been an intimate one. Largely on the basis of a questionable re-analysis of an anecdotal example which Freud uses, it has even been proposed that Minna may have had an abortion after becoming pregnant with Freud's child.)[4] Although both honesty and sexual drive were corner-stones of psychoanalysis, Freud did not openly encourage sexual freedom or permissiveness. His sons were sent to the

family doctor to learn about the facts of life and Martin recalls how his father warned him of the dangers of masturbation. In spite of his conviction of its importance, Freud sometimes referred quite disparagingly to sexuality, 'the coarse, animal need of mankind'.[5]

Another aspect of contrast is Freud's vacillation between self-confidence and doubt in his own abilities. His ambivalence towards the quality of his achievements is matched by the even greater range of opinion of others about him, from reverence for genius to belittling sarcasm. One of Freud's characteristics was his ability to stand his ground alone in the face of opposition, yet his letters reveal his delight when honours were bestowed upon him. Freud has often been accused of arrogance by those who seceded from the main stream of the psychoanalytic movement. It is true that many of his closest friendships and working relationships (as with Breuer and with Adler and Jung) ended in disputes and bitterness. But this is counterpointed by the depth and continuity of his feelings for many other of his friends and colleagues even when, like Binswanger and Rank, they had moved in their thinking outside the orthodox fold. In a charming comment in one of his letters in 1911, Freud recognizes this ambiguity in himself:

> I have always made it my principle to be tolerant and not to exercise authority, but in practice it does not always work. It is like cars and pedestrians. When I began going about by car I got just as angry at the carelessness of pedestrians as I used to be at the recklessness of drivers.[6]

It is in the nature of Freud's intellectual work that we perhaps see most clearly this quality of polarity and paradox. Freud had a high capacity for detailed and persevering work. His early anatomical investigations depended on laborious dissection and precise observations. His psychological theories also emerge from attentive and careful sifting of the fine detail of material from his patients and from his self-analysis. At the same time, his theory is notable for its bold and imaginative sweeps, often soaring well beyond what evidence there is, in its attempts to make sense of the complexities and vicissitudes of mental life. The breadth of Freud's interests were noted earlier. At one and the same time he is a scientist and an artist/philosopher. Psychoanalysis too is at once *biological* in its basis (in 1895 Freud even made a bold attempt to express it in neuroanatomical terms) and also essentially *psychological* in that it focuses on the *meaning* of psychological events both conscious and unconscious. Freud's fantasy idea of a college of psychoanalysis[7] certainly embraced a broad spectrum of subjects from biology and psychiatry to the history of civilization, mythology, religion and the study of literature.

Freud's attitude to his theory is variable. At times he takes it to be a more or less factual account. At others, he sees it as a 'mythology' – just one way of viewing personality which, in the course of time, will be replaced by a securer foundation as neurophysiology advances.

This then is a sketch of the complexities of Freud the man. We will take up this topic again in Chapter 11 which considers the influence of his life and characteristics upon his work.

CHAPTER 3

The Unconscious

One of Freud's first findings as a therapist was that the real motivation for an act may be disguised and not even apparent to the person who performs it. This is illustrated by the case of Bertha Pappenheim, the patient of his colleague Breuer, which is recorded in their joint publication *Studies in hysteria* (where Bertha is referred to as 'Anna O').

> It was in the summer during a period of extreme heat, and the patient was suffering very badly from thirst; for, without being able to account for it in any way, she suddenly found it impossible to drink. She would take up the glass of water she longed for, but as soon as it touched her lips she would push it away like someone suffering from hydrophobia. As she did this, she was obviously in an 'absence' for a couple of seconds. She lived only on fruit, such as melons, etc., so as to lessen her tormenting thirst. This had lasted for some 6 weeks, when one day during hypnosis she grumbled about her English 'lady-companion' whom she did not care for, and went on to describe, with every sign of disgust, how she had once gone into that lady's room and how her little dog – horrid creature! – had drunk out of a glass there. The patient had said nothing, as she had wanted to be polite. After giving further energetic expression to the anger she had held back, she asked for something to drink, drank a large quantity of water without any difficulty and woke from her hypnosis with the glass at her lip; and thereupon the disturbance vanished, never to return. [1]

In this case, what appeared to be the reason for Anna's refusal to drink (the act's associations with her pent-up feelings of disgust at the sight of the dog drinking from a glass and possibly also with her dislike of her companion) operated at an unconscious level. In the authors' terms, the repressed emotion had been converted into another form – her phobia about drinking. The release of feeling which came when she expressed the original episode during therapy, they described as *abreaction* and their method as *cathartic*.

In a later paper (*The Ego and the Id*, 1923)[2] Freud made the distinction between the *preconscious*, ideas and memories which an individual can bring to consciousness almost at will, and *unconscious* thought which, because of its disturbing nature, is not easily made conscious even though it may still indirectly influence behaviour. The psychoanalyst's problem is how to elicit the unconscious meaning. It is not readily obtainable by asking a patient to introspect. If the meaning is traumatic, and in the case above, there may be active resistance to making it conscious. This idea of 'inner censorship' or repression is an important feature of psychoanalytic theory as we shall see.

> What is to be understood by the censor? No entity is meant. The censor simply denotes the sum of the urges which prevail in the consciousness of a given individual, in so far as the said urges exercise an inhibitory function upon the urges opposed to them, which they drive back into the unconscious. It must however, be noted that in Freud's view this inhibitory function is only consciously exercised in very early life; it soon becomes automatic, then unconscious, and repression takes the place of suppression. Not only does the censor consign to the unconscious the urges which oppose it and which have penetrated into consciousness, but its inhibitory power is exercised even before their entry into consciousness. This is one of Freud's most highly original concepts.[3]

Freud's early efforts were focused on the problem of getting at unconscious meaning. He first tried hypnosis but soon discarded it as he realized its limitations. Not all patients could be sent into a trance of sufficient depth, nor was it always possible to get them to accept interpretations which had been elicited by bypassing their normal state of mind. He eventually developed a technique designed to relax the inner 'controls' which structure and filter the contents of consciousness and communication to the therapist. *Freier Einfall* is usually translated as *free association* though *Einfall* literally means 'a sudden idea or irruption'. The essence of free association is that patients are encouraged to express freely everything which comes into their minds and to avoid any attempt to structure their thought or to check or filter what they say aloud. This became the fundamental rule of psychoanalysis – the only rule which all patients are obliged and expected to follow at all times in therapeutic sessions. The account below by Ruth Munroe conveys well the flavour of the free association method and also something of the complexity and multiple levels of unconscious meaning.

> The patient begins with a brief report of the previous day – a sort of routine in his analytic sessions. Nothing special: he had a conference with his boss about a going project. He didn't quite like the boss's policy, but it was not too bad and who was he, in the hierarchy of his institution, to contradict the boss? By now this was an old issue in the analysis: did he habitually give in too easily, or did he evaluate correctly the major contours of his job? In any event, the conference was just a conference like any other. He'd had a dream – something about an ironing board, but that was as far as he could go.

Associations to ironing board? Well, we have one. 'Matter of fact, my wife said our maid irons badly. She could iron my shirts better herself, but I don't think she could and I'm sure she wouldn't. Anyhow, my shirts look all right to me. I wish she wouldn't worry so much. I hope she doesn't fire that maid.' The patient suddenly hums a bit from *Lohengrin* and has to hunt for the words on the request of the analyst. It is the passage where Lohengrin reveals his glorious origin. ('My father, Parsifal, wears his crown and I am his knight, Lohengrin.') Patient: 'Now I think of that last report X [his boss] turned in. That was *my* work – only I can't say so. That ironing board – my mother was ironing. I jumped off the cupboard, wonderful jump, but I sort of used her behind as support – she was leaning over. She told father I had been disrespectful and he gave me a licking. I was awfully hurt. I hadn't even thought about her old behind – it was just a wonderful jump. Father would never let me explain. My sister says he was proud of me. He never acted that way. He was awfully strict. I wish he hadn't died when I was so young – we might have worked things out.'

It is the task of the analyst to select from this material the themes most worthwhile to pursue at any given period. For us it is enough to observe that the *non sequiturs* of the patient's own job situation (where he did not *consciously* feel threatened), the ironing board, with his wife's attitude toward the maid's job, the enormous self-reassurance of the *Lohengrin* passage, and finally the resurgence of a childhood memory are all closely related.

The process is quite different from the rational consideration: 'I am worried about my job, the boss is not such a hotshot as he thinks, and I am sorry for the maid because she seems to be in the same situation.' Or, perhaps, 'My wife is as censorious and unjust as my mother,' etc. (The reader will doubtless identify other themes of deeper importance.) On the contrary, the patient would honestly deny any such concerns, at least on the occasion of an ordinary job conference. Indeed, at the time the wife–maid sequence appears, the patient has not remembered the childhood episode and is not aware that he is making more than a passing comment on a trifling domestic incident consciously considered as being outside his own sphere of interest. Far from seeking consolation in the *Lohengrin* saga consciously, he does not even realize what he is humming until the analyst asks him.[4]

Psychoanalysts consider that free association can often open up avenues to the unconscious problems of a patient. As Munroe points out, it is valuable too in that it is 'information rather easily shared with the patient himself as he too comes to recognize underlying themes'.[5] Free association is a method frequently used in psychoanalytic therapy not only on its own, but also as an adjunct to other techniques such as dream interpretation.

For Freud the 'royal road to the unconscious' was *dreams*. You have almost surely noticed yourself how, when falling asleep, the rational, reality-testing processes of the mind become relaxed. Anxieties and fantasies loom larger. What is in reality unlikely begins to seem more possible. Freud regarded *The Interpretation of Dreams*, published relatively early in his career in 1900, as his most significant book. Freud considered that dreams essentially represent wish fulfilments. Sometimes, as in the case of children's dreams of sweets and toys, the wish is portrayed directly in the content of the dream. The motivations underlying the dreams of adults are more likely to be unconscious, often originating in repressed experiences of childhood. Although the unconscious censoring mechanisms of the mind are relaxed during sleep, they are still operative to some extent. Unconscious wish fulfilment is therefore represented in disguised and distorted form. The underlying motivation will be fused with experiences and thoughts from the previous day or even events occurring during the course of the night – covers slipping off, a light switched on or indigestion. Although experiences represented in the dream may seem to be of a trivial, irrelevant nature, Freud argued that they occur because they reflect, if only indirectly, significant desires and emotions. Dream interpretation involves eliciting the *latent* content of the dream, that is, its underlying meaning, from the *manifest* content as reported by the dreamer. One of Freud's major contributions was to show the kinds of distortion that latent meaning undergoes in its translation, through what Freud called *dream-work*, into manifest content and how these distortions may be unravelled. The main distorting processes Freud distinguished as *condensation*, *displacement*, *dramatization*, *symbolization* and *secondary elaboration*. By *secondary elaboration*, Freud meant the distortions which occur due to the conscious restructuring that takes place when the dreamer recalls or reports his dream. The other processes are described briefly below.

Condensation

One common feature of dreams, as you may have noticed in recollecting dreams of your own, is their sparse quality. Freud considered that such brevity often represents a condensation of several underlying meaning and associations. So, for example, a single figure in a dream may represent two or more people known to the dreamer.

> The dream is meagre, paltry and laconic in comparison with the range and copiousness of the dream-thoughts. The dream, when written down, fills half a page; the analysis which contains the dream-thoughts, requires six, eight, twelve times as much space. The ratio varies with different dreams; but in my experience it is always of the same order.[6]

The process of condensation is illustrated by a dream reported by the psychoanalyst Theodor Reik.[7] A significant and repeated feature of a dream of one of his patients was the phrase 'I am afraid of the dog'. The patient was asked to free associate to it but could only say that 'dog' was an anagram of 'god'. Reik knew that the patient had been brought up in a very religious family, had been fervently religious himself while young but had later become an atheist. In the light of this, and his knowledge of the patient, he interpreted this feature of the dream as a condensation of three related, underlying meanings – fear of God, an attempt to conceal that fear from himself and contempt of God, the last two both being expressed by the transformation of 'God' into 'dog'.

An example added by Brill in his translation of *The interpretation of dreams* shows how complex the process of condensation may be. A whole wealth of meanings may be contained within a dream reported simply as an image.

One of my female patients dreams that *a man with a fair beard and a peculiar glittering eye is pointing to a sign-board attached to a tree which reads: uclamparia – wet.*

Analysis. – The man was rather authoritative-looking, and his peculiar glittering eye at once recalled the church of San Paolo, near Rome, where she had seen the mosaic portraits of the Popes. One of the early Popes had a golden eye (this is really an optical illusion, to which the guides usually call attention). Further associations showed that the general physiognomy of the man corresponded with her own clergyman (pope), and the shape of the fair beard recalled her doctor (myself), while the stature of the man in the dream recalled her father. All these persons stand in the same relation to her; they are all guiding and directing the course of her life. On further questioning, the golden eye recalled gold – money – the rather expensive psychoanalytic treatment, which gives her a great deal of concern. Gold, moreover, recalls the gold cure for alcoholism – Herr D., whom she would have married, if it had not been for his clinging to the disgusting alcohol habit – she does not object to anyone's taking an occasional drink; she herself sometimes drinks beer and liqueurs. This again brings her back to her visit to San Paolo (*fuori la mura*) and its surroundings. She remembers that in the neighbouring monastery of the *Tre Fontane* she drank a liqueur made of *eucalyptus* by the Trappist monks of the monastery. She then relates how the monks transformed this malarial and swampy region into a dry and wholesome neighbourhood by planting numbers of *eucalyptus* trees. The word *'uclamparia'* then resolves itself into *eucalyptus* and *malaria*, and the word *wet* refers to the former swampy nature of the locality. Wet also suggests dry. *Dry* is actually the name of the man whom she would have married but for his over-indulgence in alcohol. The peculiar name of *Dry* is of Germanic origin (*drei* – three) and hence, alludes to the monastery of the Three (*drei*) Fountains. In talking to Mr. Dry's habit she used the strong expression: 'He could drink a fountain.' Mr. Dry jocosely refers to his habit by saying: 'You know I must drink because I am always *dry*' (referring to his name). The *eucalyptus* refers also to her neurosis, which was at first diagnosed as *malaria*. She went to Italy because her attacks of anxiety, which were accompanied by marked rigors and shivering, were thought to be of malarial origin. She bought some eucalyptus oil from the monks, and she maintains that it has done her much good.

The condensation *uclamparia* – *wet* is therefore the point of junction for the dream as well as for the neurosis.[8]

Displacement

The real focus of the dream may not be where it seems to be. Displacement is where 'the dream is, as it were, centred elsewhere; its content is arranged about elements which do not constitute the central part of the dream-thoughts'.[9] One form of displacement is *substitution*. The intention underlying the dream is disguised by transferring an act or emotion on to some other person or object other than that which, in actuality, arouses the unconscious feeling. An example is provided by a dream reported by Ferenczi, a pupil of Freud's. One of his patients saw herself in a dream strangling a little white dog. Free association suggested a link between the dog and her sister-in-law. She not only had a notably pale complexion but the dreamer recalled a row which they had had a few days earlier in which she had accused her sister-in-law of being 'a dog who bites'. Using another colloquial phrase, she told Ferenczi that her annoyance stemmed from the fact that her sister-in-law was trying to come between her husband and herself 'like a tame dove'. The patient had previously associated the action of strangling the dog with wringing the neck of a chicken which she was occasionally obliged to do. To express her hostility directly in the form of a dream in which she killed her sister-in-law would be too disturbing. So, according to Ferenczi's interpretation, the underlying wish was displaced on to a disguised representation of the sister-in-law – the dog.

In Freud's view, dream-work might not only displace emotion but also suppress or even invert it. In a later edition of *The Interpretation of Dreams*, Freud cites another dream recorded by Ferenczi which illustrates this process.

An elderly gentleman was awakened at night by his wife, who was frightened because he laughed so loudly and uncontrollably in his sleep. The man afterwards related that he had the following dream: 'I lay in my bed, a gentleman known to me came in, I wanted to turn on the light, but I could not; I attempted to do so repeatedly, but in vain. Thereupon my wife got out of bed in order to help me, but she, too, was unable to manage it; being ashamed of her *négligé* in the presence of the gentleman, she finally gave it up and went back to her bed; all this was so comical that I had to laugh terribly. My wife said: "What are you laughing at, what are you laughing at?'' but I continued to laugh until I woke.' The following day the man was extremely depressed, and suffered from headache: 'From too much laughter, which shook me up' he thought.

Analytically considered, the dream looks less comical. In the latent dream-thoughts the 'gentleman known' to him who came into the room is the image of death as the 'great unknown', which was awakened in his mind on the previous day. The old gentleman, who suffers from arteriosclerosis, had good reason to think of death on the day before the dream. The uncontroll-able laughter takes the place of weeping and sobbing at the idea that he has to die. It is the light of life that he is no longer able to turn on. This mournful thought may well have associated itself with a failure to effect sexual intercourse, which he had attempted shortly before this, and in which the assistance of his wife *en négligé* was of no avail; he realized that he was already on the decline. The dream-work knew how to transform the sad idea of impotence and death into a comic scene, and the sobbing into laughter.[10]

Dramatization and Symbolization

The content of the dreams cited in illustration so far reveals the *drama-tized* or pictorial form in which unconscious feelings are expressed in dreams. Fear and contempt of God take the form of a specific phrase, hostility towards a sister-in-law is depicted as strangling a dog. Impotence and/or concern with death becomes an inability to switch on a light. Recall of your own dreams may also confirm the pictorial, dramatized concrete nature of their content. The associative links between image and feeling, as we have seen, are often personal to the dreamer and can only be uncovered with the help of other information about the patient and free association. Some images, however, are commonly found in our culture to represent significant objects, events or emotions. These are what Freud means by symbols. So he considered, for example, that objects which resemble the penis in shape (e.g., elongated things like snakes, sticks, neck-ties, trains or trees) or in function (e.g., intrusive things like guns or daggers or erective things like planes or umbrellas) may symbolically represent it. Likewise, 'small boxes, chests, cupboards and ovens correspond to the female organ; also cavities, ships and all kinds of vessels'.[11] The actions of climbing ladders, stairs, inclines or flying may be used to symbolize sexual intercourse; having a haircut, tooth pulled or being beheaded, castration. Whether a dream image is a symbol or an idiosyncratic representation personal to the dreamer can only really be determined by investigation. Dream interpretation is not possible merely by referring to some 'dictionary of symbols'. Symbols occur, of course, not only in dreams but in art, literature and the col-loquial language of daily life. So 'bread' symbolizes money, 'pulling off' masturbation, 'bun in the oven' pregnancy, the expression 'you don't look at the mantlepiece when you poke the fire' a disregard for the facial attributes of a sexual partner. If many of the examples I have chosen here have sexual connotations, this reflects (or at least I presume it does!) the fact that symbols are characteristically used when acts are 'forbidden' and where direct expression would conflict with the 'censor' or *superego* as Freud was to call it.

In 1901, the year following the issue of *The Interpretation of Dreams*, Freud published *The Psychopathology of Everyday Life*.[12] In this book he suggested that unconscious motivation could influence not only dreams, fantasy and free association but also the way in which we carry out the activities of everyday life. He devoted the book to the study of *parapraxes* – erroneous actions, slips of the tongue and forgetful behaviour which reflect underlying intent. As the concept of the Freudian slip is almost surely familiar to you, two quotations from the book may suffice to illustrate their operation (and something of the flavour of Freud's style and attitudes). The first is an example of a slip of the tongue.

> A lady once expressed herself in society – the words show that they were uttered with fervour and under the pressure of a great many secret emotions: 'Yes a woman must be pretty if she is to please the men. A man is much better off. As long as he has five straight limbs he needs no more!'
>   This example affords us a good insight into the intimate mechanisms of a mistake in speech by means of condensation and contamination. It is quite obvious that we have here a fusion of two similar modes of expression:
>   'As long as he has his four *straight limbs* . . .'
>   'As long as he has all his *five senses* . . .'
> It may also be assumed that both modes of expression . . . have cooperated to introduce into the sentence about straight limbs . . . the mysterious five instead of the simple four. But this fusion surely would not have succeeded if it had not expressed good sense in the form resulting from the mistake; if it had not expressed a cynical truth which, naturally, could not be uttered unconcealed, coming as it did from a woman.[13]

The second begins with an example from Freud's own experience.

> That accidental actions are really intentional will find no greater credence in any other sphere than in sexual activity, where the border between the intention and accident hardly seems discernible. That an apparently clumsy movement may be utilized in a most refined way for sexual purposes I can verify by a nice example from my own experience. In a friend's house I met a young girl visitor who excited in me a feeling of fondness which I had long believed extinct, thus putting me in a jovial, loquacious and complaisant mood. At that time I endeavoured to find out how this came about, as a year ago this same girl made no impression on me.

As the girl's uncle, a very old man entered the room, we both jumped to our feet to bring him a chair which stood in the corner. She was more agile than I and also nearer the object, so that she was first to take possession of the chair. She carried it with its back to her, holding both hands on the edge of the seat. As I got there later and did not give up the claim to carrying the chair, I suddenly stood directly back of her, and with both my arms was embracing her from behind, and for a moment my hands touched her lap. I naturally solved the situation as quickly as it came about. Nor did it occur to anybody how dexterously I had taken advantage of this awkward movement.

Occasionally I have had to admit to myself that the annoying awkward stepping aside on the street, whereby for some seconds one steps here and there, yet always in the same direction as the other person until finally both stop facing each other, that this 'barring one's way' repeats an ill-mannered, provoking conduct of earlier times and conceals erotic purposes under the mask of awkwardness. From my psychoanalysis of neurotics I know that the so-called *naïveté* of young people and children is frequently only such a mask employed in order that the subject may say or do the indecent without restraint.

W. Stekel has reported similar observations in regard to himself: 'I entered a house and offered my right hand to the hostess. In a most remarkable way I thereby loosened the bow which held together her loose morning-gown. I was conscious of no dishonourable intent, still I executed this awkward movement with the agility of a juggler'.[14]

'Parapraxis' was the word coined by Freud's translators for his original term *Fehlleistung*. This is a combination of two everyday German words and is better translated, Bettelheim has suggested, as 'faulty achievement'. Its rendering as 'parapraxis' has an altogether more abstract and theoretical ring. This is one of many examples which Bettelheim[15] cites of the distortions introduced into our appreciation of Freud when we read him in translation.

Fehlleistungen offer another important source of data to the psychoanalyst. He will observe his patients' words and behaviour carefully and sift their accounts of their activities for hints of their unconscious meaning. Continuous late arrival for the analytic session, for example, might indicate hostility or resentment towards the analyst. An impressive sequence of 'accidental' mishaps might indicate aggression against the self.

The analyst's primary skill and art is interpretation, eliciting the meaning underlying a person's behaviour and experience. Reik has called this process 'listening with the third ear'. The analyst feels for the underlying themes. Interpretation of the first two or three manifestations, be they dreams, free associations or behaviour, are inevitably tentative, no more than working hypotheses to be matched against further evidence. Gradually, consistencies may begin to appear. If only seen as through a glass darkly, a pattern emerges. Psychoanalytic interpretation is rather like doing a jigsaw in which one can never be sure that all the pieces are there!

CHAPTER 4

Psychosexual Development

In 1905, Freud produced his paper 'Jokes and their relation to the unconscious'. He regarded jokes as in some ways analogous to dreams (it was
this similarity that had prompted his friend Fliess to suggest to Freud
that he write about them). A joke does not express its meaning directly
but usually presents it in abbreviated or distorted form or as a set of
clues. The joke comes when the listener draws the appropriate inference
and the latent meaning becomes apparent.

In the same year, Freud also published his *Three Essays on Sexuality*,
perhaps the most important of his books after *The Interpretation of
Dreams*. In the course of his work with Breuer, Freud had formed the
conclusion that some kind of sexual disturbance invariably underlay
hysterical neurosis. In this book, he explored the complex nature and
significance of sexuality and its relationship with personality development. In particular, he put forward the original proposal that sexual
development takes place within the first five years of life and that what
happens then is of crucial significance for the later adult – not just in
terms of sexual life but character as well. Freud was stressing the significance of *ontogenetic* development (the origins and development of the
individual). If we want to understand the adult, then we need to retrace
his childhood development. Freud's realization of the tremendous importance of childhood, particularly the first five years of life, is one of his
most important insights and one which has been amply vindicated by
subsequent research of varied kinds on both humans and other species.[1]

Quite *why* the first five years have such impact is not easily determined. Some possible reasons were suggested in Chapter 1. The work of
Piaget indicates that the nature of the young child's experience is qualitatively different from that of the adult. We might expect his world to be
less stable and ordered, more intensely coloured by his fears and hopes.
His defences against fear and anxiety are primitive and undeveloped.
With his more restricted time perspective, the immediate situation
assumes dramatic prominence. For all these reasons, an event perceived
as relatively insignificant by an adult may have lasting and telling effects

in the experience of a young child. The phenomenon of 'imprinting' has been found to occur in the young of several species, particularly birds. It refers to a critical and limited period during development when the young bird is specially predisposed to certain kinds of learning, for example to follow a particular large moving object (which would usually, of course, be the parent). Once imprinting has been established, it is not easy to reverse. Bowlby's[2] work on attachment has suggested that in humans also early childhood is a time of special sensitivity for emotional learning.

Freud believed that we do not easily acknowledge the significance of childhood events because of *infantile amnesia*. When experiences are painful or frustrating they are repressed and leave only relatively unimportant *screen memories* – the isolated episodes which we can recall. These are rather like the manifest content of a dream and have to be worked on to get at the latent meaning in the unconscious. There may be active resistance to this and Freud attributes the reluctance of his contemporaries (and even in himself) to accept the notion of infantile sexuality to such resistance.

Freud conceived of development as a complex interaction between a biologically-programmed timetable of development and the environment and social context of the child. To describe the biological component he used the concept of *Trieb* which is usually translated as instinct or drive. In Freud's use of the term, drives have their *source* in the bodily structure and functioning of the organism. They also have an *aim* which is a somatic modification or bodily gratification of some kind which is experienced as satisfaction. Drives also have an *object* which is instrumental in providing gratification. This is modifiable as a result of learning and experience. In effect then, instincts or drives are conceptualized as tension systems arising from bodily functioning. All psychic energy arises from the operation of the drives.

Even as a student, Freud had been attracted by Darwin's *Origin of Species*, which had appeared three years after his birth, and, although he does not directly relate his conception of drive to evolutionary theory, it is consistent with it. Initially, Freud classified drives into two basic types. He used the term 'ego instincts' to refer to those drives which promote preservation of the self. Hunger and thirst come into this category. The 'sexual instincts' denote, in contrast, those drives whose effect is preservation of the species. Later, in *Beyond the Pleasure Principle* (1920),[3] he developed a somewhat different dichotomy. He grouped together both ego and sexual instincts calling them *Eros* or the life drives. In opposition to Eros he postulated the death instinct (sometimes called *Thanatos*). By the death instinct, Freud meant an urge to self-destruction. This he regarded as a manifestation of a conservative tendency inherent in all vital processes – to return to an earlier state. *'The aim of all life is death . . . inanimate things existed before living ones . . .'*[4] The death instinct may express itself in potentially self-destructive behaviour – taking unnecessary risks, drug or alcohol addiction and attempts at suicide. Like the sexual drive, Freud considered that the death instinct can also express itself in indirect ways. Thus, it might be directed outwards in the form of aggression against others.

Though he later came to accept its existence as fact, when he initially suggested it, Freud admitted that his concept of the death instinct was highly speculative. It is certainly dependent on some rather dubious reasoning. It has proved to be very much a point of contention and is not accepted by many contemporary analysts. Freud's colleague and biographer, Ernest Jones, has suggested that Freud's personal concern with death may have played a part in stimulating this idea. He first introduced the death instinct shortly after the First World War when he was in his sixties. He did suffer some trouble from a heart complaint, and at one time, when he had been superstitiously preoccupied with predicting the date of his own death, he had believed that this would be when he reached 62. The notion of a 'compulsion to repeat' from which his reasoning about the tendency to return to a previous state stemmed, was based not only on his observation that patients kept coming back in their fantasies to painful experiences, but also from watching his grandson Ernst. A frequent game of his was to repeatedly throw a toy out of sight and then retrieve it. Freud interpreted this as a way of symbolically gaining control over the feeling of loss occasioned by the temporary absences of his mother. (Ernst's mother was Sophie, Freud's second daughter who died in January of the year in which *Beyond the Pleasure Principle* was published).

Freud considered the development and functioning of *libido* (as he called the sexual drive) to be of particular significance for the personality of an individual. Survival depends on fairly immediate gratification of ego instincts. If a child does not eat and drink he cannot live. The goals of these drives, i.e., the form of gratification they require, are therefore relatively fixed and there is little variation possible in the way they are expressed. Libido or sexual drive, in contrast, is infinitely more malleable. Individual survival is not jeopardized by lack of gratification. Considerable variation is possible both in the objects of libidinal drive and the ways in which it can be expressed. Environment and social context, as well as biological development, come to play an important role in determining their form and expression.

Freud's use of the term 'sexual' is distinct from everyday usage. For Freud, libido is essentially a drive whose object is the stimulation of various bodily areas, or 'erotogenic zones'. He considered psychosexual development to advance through a biologically pre-set sequence. The first phase of development takes place over the first five years of life. This phase encompasses several stages, each associated both with a particular erotogenic zone and with a particular 'mode' or means of achieving gratification. The degree and kind of satisfaction which the child experiences at each stage will depend very much on his interactions with those who nurture him. According to Freudian theory, either excessive gratification or frustration will have abiding consequences for the individual. The nature of the consequences will be a function of the stage at which frustration or indulgence occurred and the forms which they took. They will help to determine not only the style of sexual satisfactions sought by that person as an adult but also his personality and characteristic emotional reactions.

Initially, the infant's zone of interest is the mouth, his mode of satisfaction, sucking. As teeth develop, so pleasure comes from biting. In these first *oral* stages, the infant's primary psychological orientation is one of incorporation. He seeks to take in aspects of the world which he encounters. His role is largely passive in that his essential well-being depends almost entirely on the actions of others. If his needs are satisfied, he comes to conceive of existence in a positive way and to see the world about him as warm and benevolent. If he is deprived, his emotional orientation may well be pessimistic; he may come to anticipate that the world will be unrewarding and hostile to his needs. Freud assumed that 'fixation' at this stage, as a result of either deprivation or overgratification, is likely to result in an adult who is overly concerned with oral gratification. This may take the form of sucking or chewing sweets, smoking, drinking or even excessive talking. Or fixation may express itself in over-use of the modes of action associated with this stage – passivity, dependency, concern with incorporating the values, the 'goodness' of others.

As children grow older, become mobile and develop the capacity to communicate with their parents, the zone of interest shifts to the anus. Pleasure comes through retention and elimination of faeces 'which act as a stimulating mass upon a sexually sensitive portion of the mucous membrane'.[5] This *anal* stage has important implications for the relationship between infant and parent, and Freudian analysts consider that the foundation for key personality characteristics is laid down at this stage. In the course of toilet training the child is required to gain control over his bowel movements and to excrete only at the proper time and place. His stools 'are clearly treated as a part of the infant's body and represent his first 'gift': by producing them he can express his active compliance with his environment and, by withholding them, his disobedience'.[6] In response to the demands made upon him, he can submit, rebel or learn to cope with authority while maintaining his own autonomy. In a later paper, Freud (1908)[7] explored in some detail the various traits that can depend on this stage. If the pleasure a child takes in playing with his faeces is severely constrained by his parents, for example, he may develop defences against such forbidden pleasures which may express themselves later as obsessive orderliness and cleanliness. If parents reinforce his production on the potty, this may lay the foundation for later pleasure in creating. And miserliness may result from a child developing an unwillingness to 'let go'.

In the third or *phallic* stage, the child of 4 or 5 years turns the focus of his attention to the genitals. Sexual differences assume significance. Contact with children of the opposite sex may arouse curiosity. The young child is likely to enjoy masturbation or arousal situations like bath-time or being bumped up and down on an adult's knee. Up to this point, Freud argues that psychosexual development has been much the same for both the sexes. At this stage, however, their developmental paths diverge. The natural feelings of affection felt by the boy for his mother may now be intensified and coloured by the erotic feelings aroused by masturbation. He is likely to desire close contact, like sleeping beside her at night, and show sexual curiosity about her. Such intensified feelings are complicated by feelings of rivalry with his father which may arouse in the child both fear and hostility. The young boy may be afraid of loss of love and even castration, given his focus of interest on the penis and his still largely autistic (i.e., fantasy-determined) view of reality. This conflict Freud called the Oedipus complex. Freud supposed this to be universal. He considered it no coincidence that parricide is the theme not only of Sophocles' *Oedipus Rex* but also of two other masterpieces of literature, Shakespeare's *Hamlet* and Dostoevsky's *The Brothers Karamazov*. However, anthropological evidence suggests that it is more likely a feature of a particular style of family structure, such as the patriarchal pattern of Freud's own time, common in certain cultures but not all. The idea certainly had a personal foundation. In his self-analysis and interpreting his own dreams, he had been surprised at the hostility and guilt he had discovered in relation to his father and the almost erotic nature of his feelings for his mother.

The way the boy handles this conflict again helps determine the sexual and emotional patterns of later life. Satisfactory adjustment may be made by intensified identification with his father. One consequence of this identification, according to Freud, is introjection of parental attitudes and prohibitions, thus providing the basis for conscience or *superego*. It also lays the foundation for appropriate sex role behaviour in later life and may influence the nature of adult sexual relationships. For example, intense ambivalence towards the mother may be created if conflict between the boy's desire for her and his jealousy and fear of his father, is extreme. He may resolve this by over-idealizing her and repressing the sexual feelings she arouses in him. This may make it difficult later for him to integrate affection and sexual need. Women come to be reacted to in one of two ways – either idealized or regarded as fit only for sex. This pattern was evident in extreme form in a psychiatrist I once knew. Although he enjoyed sex with prostitutes and at one stage with a mistress, he was never able to consummate his marriage. Although he was physically attracted to his wife, he found himself impotent with her.

Freud's account of the psychosexual development of girls at this stage* is more sketchy and controversial. He argued that a key experience is the sense of loss when a girl realizes that she has no penis. With the growing realization that she is not alone in this, that neither her mother nor any other female possesses a penis, she comes emotionally to devalue all women. Up to this point, like the boy, the girl's focus of affection has been the mother. Penis envy serves to shift her interest and affection to her father. Freud considered that fantasies of pregnancy or even desire to possess or rival men my represent unconsciously and symbolically attempts to acquire the 'missing' part. Many psychoanalysts (e.g. Jones) and others, however, have criticized Freud's concept of penis envy as too 'phallocentric'.[9]

At about the age of five, sexual development enters a period of latency where direct expression is constricted by the gradual emergence, encouraged by education, of opposing mental forces such as shame, disgust and moral and aesthetic ideals. Sexual energy is diverted into affection. Freud believed that this latency period was a necessary condition for the development of advanced civilization as well as a significant factor in predisposition to neurosis.

Sexual feelings re-emerge at puberty. They are now no longer largely auto-erotic but are likely to involve a search for a partner. Both sensual and affectionate expression is fused in a sexual act which is focused on genital stimulation. (Other infantile modes are quite likely to be present but, in normal development, are essentially subordinated in the role of fore-pleasure.) Infantile psychosexual development now bears its fruit. Freud explained sexual perversions (i.e., where satisfaction is achieved *primarily* from oral or anal as opposed to genital contact) as being due to a fixation at (or regression to) one or another of the infantile stages, as a result of either frustration *or* overgratification at that time. According to Freud, neuroses are merely the 'negative of perversions'.[10] Where there is fixation on infantile needs but where these have been repressed and so prevented from direct expression, they may take the form of neurotic symptoms. Emotional patterns are also transferred to the adult situation. So if, for example, there had been strong sibling rivalry, this may well lead the person as an adult to be very competitive with colleagues or even to stir up similar rivalry among his or her own children. Personality characteristics emerge in a similar way. Emphasis on an infantile *mode* rather than zone of gratification may result, as we have seen, in a predisposition towards dependency, optimism, obsessiveness, creativity, rebelliousness, submissiveness, etc., in varied degrees and complex combinations. For Freud, perversion, neurosis and character are but different orchestrations of the same theme.

CHAPTER 5

Psychodynamics

As described so far, Freudian theory suggests a *dynamic*, purposive conception of the person. There is a basic driving urge to satisfy instinctual need which provides the source of all psychic energy. It is also a conception which stresses the significance of *conflict* and the ways in which an individual seeks to balance the various forces acting upon and within him. If direct attainment of satisfaction is blocked either because of external restraints or because of inner censorship by conflicting feelings internalized as a result of identification with significant others in the child's life such as parents, this energy may seek some other form of expression – in fantasy, dreams or unconsciously influencing the form of actions. Thirdly, Freudian theory emphasizes the significance of *development* and the often abiding consequences of conflicts and experiences in early life.

In his later writings, the focus of Freud's interests shifted from libido theory, psychosexual development and the operations of the unconscious to social and philosophical issues and, in particular, the processes of inner conflict and integration. This development, often called *ego psychology*, has been subsequently elaborated upon by later psycho-analysts. It has particular relevance to this book in that our focus of interest is on the individual as integrator.

In *The Ego and the Id* (1923)[1] Freud drew together ideas initiated in earlier works and presented a more formalized conceptualization of the psyche or mind as an energy system taking the form of a confluence of interacting forces which may, and often do, conflict. These forces, Freud suggested, were broadly of three types. The most basic and primitive of these he called the *id*. The id is the source of all instinctual energy and is rooted in the biological characteristics of the human species. Such energy is dynamic. Its 'discharge' either through consummatory actions or appropriate fantasy is experienced as *pleasure*. Where discharge is blocked, that is, where the urge cannot be directly gratified in action or fantasy, tension results. According to Freudian theory, the young baby is dominated by id impulses. If such needs are not met, tension builds up.

He screams until breast or bottle are produced or his nappy is changed. Once he is gratified, tension is relieved and he rests back content.

As the child grows older, his perceptual and motor abilities develop. He is able gradually to 'internalize' or to build up a conception of his external world. He is no longer merely a passive recipient, he can act upon this world. In conjunction with pleasure, another principle comes into operation to direct experience and behaviour – the *reality principle*. This aspect of self, the *ego*, mediates between the individual and the external world. Like the id, it also is concerned with obtaining pleasure but because it is capable of reflecting the conditions of the outside world, it is tempered as well by concern for gratification within the bounds of reality. Ego forces represent the cognitive and perceptual capacities of a person. Past events and future consequences can be taken into account. Going for immediate gratification could, in some circumstances, for example, put survival at risk. And in many situations, maximum pleasure may be best obtained by postponing immediate gratification. Not going out tonight enables you to put the money you would have spent towards having an even better time when you go on holiday. Thus, although id and ego both serve the same end (pleasure), by sometimes seeking to postpone immediate gratification the ego may conflict with id.

As the infant becomes the young child, he is generally required by parents, other adults and sometimes older children, to mould his behaviour in particular ways. Initially this is likely to be a process of direct control through reinforcement and/or punishment. As the infant grows older, he also begins to distinguish between himself and the other significant people in his world. As part of normal development, a child is likely to *identify* with one or other parent or consistent adult figure in his life. As a result, the child imitates, incorporates within himself, as it were, certain of their key characteristics. In particular, as discussed in the previous section, he is likely at the Oedipal phase to 'introject' or internalize their injunctions and demands. In other words, a child begins to develop a *superego* or conscience. Immediate control by others may then no longer be necessary. The child has incorporated their demands as part of the identification process. Control is now internal. The superego becomes an important source of inner conflict as moral teaching and the demands made by parents in western society are frequently in opposition to instinctual needs.

It is important to note that Freud did not mean to imply that id, ego and superego are identifiable processes in the human brain. Rather they are conceptualizations or abstractions used to refer to the interacting forces which govern behaviour: one of instinctual, hereditary origin; the others both a function of learning, in the case of the ego, learning the 'realities' which govern action and experience, in the case of the superego assimilation of key aspects of the cultural and familial context in which a child is reared. As noted earlier, one of the problems with reading Freud in English is the shift in meaning that can come about through translation from German. 'Ego' is the usual translation of the word used by Freud – *das Ich*. This ordinary German personal pronoun means literally 'the I'. It carries an entirely different set of connotations from the use of the word 'ego'. It is not a quasi-scientific term. Nor does it convey any sense of self-centredness or self-importance as ego may often do in English. By using *das Ich* Freud firmly anchors this aspect of the psyche in our conscious awareness of ourselves. His original term for the id was *das Es*, literally 'the it'. This effectively puts across the notion of a different kind of impulsion capable of acting outside and sometimes in spite of our conscious intention. Bettelheim claims the effect of *das Es* is further strengthened because in German, the word child (*das Kind*) is of neuter gender:

> During their early years, all Germans have the experience of being referred to by means of the neuter pronoun *Es*. This fact gives the phrase *das Es* a special feeling, reminding the German reader that this is how he was referred to before he learned to repress many of his sexual, aggressive, and otherwise asocial impulses, before he felt guilty or ashamed because of them, before he felt an obligation to resolve contradictions and bring logical order into his thoughts; in short, it reminds him of a time when his entire existence was dominated by the It. These memories, even when he is not conscious of them, permit a much more immediate empathy with what Freud meant when he used this term for the unconscious.[2]

Superego is also a term which was introduced by Freud's English translators. His original phrase, *Über-Ich* or the 'Above-I', conveys much better the sense of an agency of control which is at the same time integrally related to the self. As Bettelheim puts it, 'Where Freud selected a word that, used in daily parlance, makes us feel vibrantly alive, the translations present us with a term from a dead language that reeks of erudition precisely when it should emanate vitality.'[3] Bettelheim argues that Freud's English translators were biased towards presenting his ideas in a more abstract and spuriously scientific and medical style than was found in the original German. Thus *Mutterleib* (mother's womb) becomes translated as 'uterus'. Where Freud writes literally of the structure of the soul it is rendered as 'mental apparatus'. In this way the emotional meanings of the original concepts are often excised in translation. As Freud used language carefully and elegantly to express the intangibilities of the mind, essential qualities of his thought can easily be obscured in translation. One effect of the translators' bias, Bettelheim claims, can be to distance us from his ideas. They can all too easily become a formalized system for exploring the behaviour of others rather than living tools which can help us to gain insights into our own experience. Certainly, in reading Freud in translation, we need to be alert to the possibility that we are not encountering his ideas precisely in the way that he originally expressed them.

As indicated in the preceding discussion, the forces represented by the concepts id, ego and superego are often likely to conflict. An adolescent, for example, may feel sexual desire and wish to relieve this through masturbation. But he or she has been taught, perhaps, that masturbation is evil, perhaps even that it could cause harm. So both superego and ego (which is a function of the way that a person perceives reality even though that perception, as here, may not be valid) in this case oppose the drive.

In his later formulations, Freud considered that one consequence of intrapsychic conflict is the experience of *Angst*. (While this is translated as 'anxiety', it conveys perhaps a more pervasive sense of fear and anguish and is not, as anxiety is, necessarily directed at what may happen in the future.) The ego embodies perceptual and cognitive processes. It is in the middle of any conflict, confronted as it is by the need to balance instinctual demands from the id, moral demands of the superego and perceived dangers in the environment. The ego, therefore, becomes the focus of such anxiety.

In order to reduce anxiety, the ego seeks to ameliorate conflict and to integrate in whatever ways are possible the varied forces acting within the person. Scattered throughout Freud's writings, there are references to defensive processes whose aim is to ward off conflict. In *The Interpretation of Dreams*, for example, as we have seen, unconscious feelings may be expressed in distorted form – displaced or symbolized – in order to avoid anxiety created by conflict with the censor or superego processes. The defences assumed by the ego to resolve intrapsychic conflict are analogous to these. Freud discussed defence mechanisms directly in some of his later papers.[4] It was left to later psychoanalysts, however, in particular Freud's daughter Anna, to develop a more formalized conception of the ego and its 'mechanisms of defence'. Although 'defence mechanism' is the term normally used, it has, perhaps, too substantive a ring about it. The concept refers to a *process*; a device whereby conflict can be avoided. There is no finite number of such processes, and, as defence mechanisms are not tangible but are essentially conceptualizations, the distinction between one or other defensive process is not always clear-cut and one process may have more than one form. Anna Freud noted that her father had suggested nine varieties. In her book, *The Ego and Mechanisms of Defence* (1936),[5] she extended the list by five more. Other analysts have made further contributions.

The most pervasive and significant of all defence mechanisms is *repres-*

sion. Impulses which in some way are disturbing are shut out of consciousness. Freud was using this idea to explain his patients' symptoms as early as his studies with Breuer on hysteria (1895). You will remember he accounted for Bertha Pappenheim's hydrophobia as due to the disgust she had repressed on seeing her companion's dog drinking from a glass. Another patient described in that book whose case provides a further illustration of repression is Fraülein Elizabeth von R. She complained of severe pains in her legs and found it difficult to stand or walk for any length of time. After many sessions, her story gradually emerged and Freud was able to relate her symptoms to two events in her past. She had spent several years devotedly caring for her sick father who subsequently died. The pains occurred at the spot where he had rested his legs on hers while she changed his dressings. Eventually she revealed that she had felt at the time that her filial devotion had interfered with a potentially important relationship she had begun with a young man. The second episode concerned her brother-in-law. Some years later, at a time when Elizabeth was much preoccupied with her own need for love, her sister had been taken seriously ill. At her sister's insistence, she had taken a walk in the woods with her husband to whom she was attracted. So much had Elizabeth enjoyed their conversation that she returned to the same spot a few days later and day-dreamed of finding a relationship of her own with a man like him. In analysis, Elizabeth recalled that when her sister had later died, she had thought that her brother-in-law would now be free to marry her. All this was remembered only with great difficulty. Freud believed that it was the repression of these guilty thoughts which caused such *resistance* and had led to the symptoms in the first place.

It is important to distinguish repression from suppression. In repression, the individual has no consciousness of his need. In suppression, on the other hand, he may not act on it but he is aware of his desire. As we have seen, repressed impulses may break through in disguised form in fantasy, dreams and behaviour. The form these expressions take is often related to the original conflict. Elizabeth's leg pains, as well as causing her pain as 'penance' for her guilty wishes, symbolically inhibited both tending her father and walking in the woods with her brother-in-law.

Cathexis is the English neologism devised by Freud's translators to denote the psychic energy invested in a desire, relationship or object. Drives which create conflict are held in check by the formation of an *anti-cathexis* – energy used to repress them. Although this prevents them entering consciousness, other defensive processes are likely to be used in support.

Another mechanism we have already encountered is *displacement*. The impulse is redirected towards a more acceptable target. An example of this is provided by a case of Anna Freud's. As a girl, this patient, who was a middle child with several brothers and sisters, suffered greatly from both jealousy and penis envy. The fierce hostility this engendered towards her mother conflicted violently with her feelings of affection. She feared, too, that the naughty behaviour which resulted from her negative feelings would make her mother angry and lead her to withdraw her love. As she grew older, she sought to alleviate her conflict by *displacement*. She always made sure there was another significant woman in her life, towards whom she could redirect the hatred she felt.

One kind of displacement which psychoanalysts consider to be of fundamental significance both for the adjustment of an individual and the development of civilization, is *sublimation*. Freud had made reference to this as early as 1905 in the *Three Essays on Sexuality*. Sublimation is the displacement of libido to non-sexual ends in a way which not only avoids conflict but actively promotes the individual's adjustment to his social context. So, according to Freud, intellectual curiosity, appreciation of beauty, love, friendship and creativity represent sublimations. The form sublimation takes will depend not only on the outlets made available by the nature of the social context, but also on the stage at which significant conflicts were aroused. Sublimations stemming from oral conflicts, for example, might take the form of lecturing or selling; at the anal stage, creative 'messing' with clay or paints, going into banking or even, perhaps, becoming a sewage operative; at the phallic stage, academic or scientific curiosity.

When displacement proved inadequate as an effective way of handling her unacceptable hostility, Anna Freud's patient, mentioned above, next resorted to *turning the hostility against herself*. Throughout her childhood and adolescence and into adult life, she was subject to self-criticism and feelings of inferiority and allowed others to make demands on her. When this too turned out to be insufficient to allay anxiety, she began to project her hostility on to others, seeing the women in her life as hating and rejecting her. *Projection* then is when unconscious drives, repressed because they clash with internalized values, are projected on to others. It is of particular interest to social psychologists. There is some evidence[6] that it may underlie some forms of prejudice. Repressed desires are projected on to the targets of prejudice, usually those who are seen by the prejudiced person as different in some way, for example, in race, religion or life-style. Thus, rampant lust may be unrealistically attributed to respectable, middle-class blacks; reckless promiscuity to meek, inhibited students. Projection is often a particularly effective means of defence in that it may offer, like a compromise, the opportunity for partial expression. The projector can quite 'justifiably' dwell upon and concern himself with the nefarious activities of others and, in doing so, achieve a degree of vicarious satisfaction without the complication of guilt. He could regard it as only 'reasonable' that a campaigner against pornography should, in order to decide what to protect the public from, view the very films and books she would ban.

Such *compromise*, where the same behaviour serves both at the same time to inhibit and to express the disturbing desire, is often seen as a defence mechanism in its own right. Ruth Munroe[7] recalls her old 'school teacher' as a nice example of this. This lady spent much of her life having to care for her aging but still lecherous father, and was afflicted by a nervous tic which took the form of a provocative wink. While this may be taken, Munroe argues, as symbolic of unconscious sexual desire, at the same time it was clearly an affliction and thus no fault of her own. There were other psychological advantages. Because the tic was unattractive, it helped protect her from the temptation of sexual involvement. Her disfigurement acted too as a punishment to assuage her guilt over her repressed desire.

The illustrations convey, I hope, something of the transformations which analysts consider desires can undergo when they arouse conflict. They may even be turned into their opposite. In *reaction formation*, a repressed impulse is held in check by exaggerating the opposite tendency. Thus an extremely gentle and unassertive personality may merely represent a way of coping with strong aggressive feelings which arouse unconscious fear of retaliation or conflict with moral ideals. A reaction formation can be detected by the excessive character of the reactive behaviour and also because, when the person is off-guard, impulses may show through. Our gentle, unassuming person may unexpectedly show a nasty side. In some cases, oscillation may occur between the reactive behaviour and direct expression of the original wish. For example, where fixation at the anal stage has occurred, periods of excessive tidiness and concern for cleanliness may be punctuated by bouts of chaotic disorder. A feature of psychoanalysis is the way the theory allows for the close coexistence of opposites; hate may mask love, and sadism easily reverse into masochism.

One way of making up a quarrel is for both parties to agree that 'it never happened'. Of course, the gesture is symbolic and it is unlikely in fact that either will really forget the event. The defence mechanism of *denial*, on the other hand, involves a genuine blindness to a frustrating aspect of reality. As Anna Freud points out, this is a common defence of children in their fantasies and sometimes their actions. Little Hans, one of her father's most well-known case studies,[8] illustrates both denial and the way defences tend to be used in concert. It was difficult for the five-year-old to go outside his house because of his deep fear that horses wanted to bite him. This was interpreted as a defence against the anxiety aroused by Oedipal conflict. His aggressive feelings towards his father were *displaced* on to horses and *reversed* so that they became a source of anxiety for him. There was also *regression* to the oral level of his fear of being bitten. After his phobia had been alleviated as a result of analysis by his own father working with the advice of Freud, Hans still had to come to terms with his feeling of inferiority in relation to his father and envy of the attention paid by his mother to his baby sister. Two of his day-dreams indicate how he tried to do this by denying these realities in fantasy. In one, the plumber came and took away Hans' penis and buttocks with pincers and gave him new and bigger ones. In the other, he imagined looking after his own children, coping with his jealousy by seeing himself in his mother's role. Play and fantasy have been seen by Freud's followers to be a very important means by which a child can work through his or her anxieties and conflicts.[9]

As an example of *denial in action and words*, Anna Freud describes the reaction of a very young girl when she realized that, unlike her two brothers, she possessed no penis. Instead of working through her concern by taking an interest in fine clothes as a substitute for display, or competing in physical activities, she denied the fact by compulsively lifting up her skirt to display her non-existent organ. This denial generalized to other behaviours – saying things were there ('look at the eggs the hens have laid!') when they were not.

In children, *denial* can be an acceptable way of coming to terms with disturbing emotions. It is not however confined to them. Years ago, my next-door neighbour would often set the table, dress up and inform us that her sister, who had died some time before, was coming to tea that afternoon. Although such explicit denial in word and actions by adults is likely to be regarded as psychotic, in more diluted form it is normal enough. The fox who, because he could not reach the grapes, decided that they must be sour and so he did not want them after all, was reinterpreting reality to fit his needs. This also might be taken as an example of *rationalization*, where an action or an impulse which has been acted out is reinterpreted so that it is seen as 'justifiable' and no longer causes the inner conflict which would be created by consciousness of its real underlying meaning.

A more sophisticated form of denial is seen in what Anna Freud has called *restriction of the ego*. In this case, painful realities are avoided, not by denying them, but by withdrawing from situations where painful confrontation is likely to occur. She describes how she had been doing some drawing with a young boy patient of hers, an activity he very much liked, when suddenly he refused to continue. She attributes this to his painful realization that in some way her drawing was better than his. He avoided this pain by refusing to draw any more. This was a pattern she later observed he often adopted when confronted by competition with others. Another example she gives is of a little girl going to her first eagerly anticipated dance. There she fell in love with a handsome boy and began to weave a web of fantasy about the relationship they might have. But while dancing, he teased her clumsiness. From then on, she avoided all opportunities to dance and dress up and came to despise this side of her. The rebuff had such impact because it represented a repetition of a traumatic situation which had happened in early childhood when she had suffered because of feelings of being unable to compete.

Anxiety aroused by conflict may also be assuaged by ritual *undoing*. The common superstitious custom of throwing salt over your shoulder to undo the 'harm' caused by spilling it could be considered to be an explicit example. On an unconscious level, carefully avoiding the cracks in the pavement or excessive handwashing may represent ways of symbolically 'undoing' or expiating disturbing impulses. Lady Macbeth's washing of hands while walking in her sleep, symbolically signifying her wish to 'undo' the murder of the king, is a classic literary example of undoing. Confession in the Catholic Church might be considered as an example of it in institutionalized form.

With the defence process of *isolation*, the impulse is allowed into awareness but is stripped of its emotional significance. Because of such a defence, in analysis it is not sufficient for a patient to be intellectually aware of the meaning of his symptoms, he has to acknowledge this on an emotional level. In extreme form, isolation is a process which can characterize murderers of the Yorkshire Ripper type. The impulse is expressed in dramatic action of a stereotyped, ritualized form. The murderer is able to divorce himself sufficiently from the emotional significance of his action so that he can contemplate what he has done with detachment and, between murders, live a normal existence.

Identification may serve as a means of defence in some circumstances. Anna Freud, for example, has described the process of *identification with an aggressor* as a way of coping with overwhelming threat. A child terrified of a gloomy landing, may pluck up courage to cross it in the dark by pretending to be a ghost himself. Bettelheim, a psychoanalyst who was himself incarcerated in a concentration camp for several years, noticed such identification among certain prisoners. Some took great pride in modelling their behaviour and appearance on the characteristics of their guards, eagerly collecting scraps of their clothing, imitating their gait and posture, adopting their value and leisure interests.[10] Possibly, an analogous process underlies the often reported phenomenon of hostages becoming involved with their captors. On of several hostages held at gunpoint for a week by a Palestinian and three other convicts in Scheveningen Prison in Holland in October 1974, was reported as saying afterwards: 'It sounds silly but we all grew to like the convicts over the days. They had been so good to us and none of us wanted to turn Koudache in.' There have been many other similar cases. A girl clerk held hostage in a Stockholm bank said when she was released that she would marry the man who had held her hostage. In another case, a girl hostage of her own accord shielded from police fire the man who had held her.[11]

It should not be assumed that defence mechanisms are inherently pathological. In some form, they pervade the fabric of our everyday lives. We may forget to pay that annoying bill, be over-polite to a person we dislike or displace irritation from the individual who arouses it to a less threatening or more innocuous target such as the cat! But even in the context of intrapsychic conflicts, defence mechanisms are, in a sense, adaptive. In the long run they may prove more of a problem than a solution, but in the short term they ameliorate inner conflicts and assuage anxiety.

What particularly interests the psychoanalyst are those defences which are rooted in the character and past of an individual. To see clearly their significance, it may be necessary to dig down through several levels. An elderly acquaintance of mine illustrates this. A feature of her behaviour which particularly troubled her family was her paranoid concern that people were talking about her and exploiting her name and their know-ledge of her to make money. These feelings were focused on doctors and her optician. She believed that her old GP, who had since passed away, had masterminded the campaign and had given her pills which damaged her throat and still affected her. Discussions with her on several occasions suggested that this pattern was related to an incident many years before when her husband had asked her to query a medical bill with the doctor. She had followed his request but only with great conflict and embarrass-ment. Knowledge of her early background and the very difficult relation-ship she had experienced with her father, made it seem probable that the basis for such conflict had been laid in childhood. The need then to repress fear of and hostility towards her father created in her case a lasting predisposition to guilt and the projection of hostility. This was resuscitated later when she found herself in a minor conflict with a figure symbolizing an authoritarian father.

Although chronological classification of defence mechanisms cannot be carried very far, it does seem likely that different defence mechanisms tend to assume prominence and to be appropriate at different stages of development. Thus, as we have seen, *denial* is a quite normal mode of defence in a young child whose reality testing is as yet at a fairly rudi-mentary stage, but such a fantasy solution would give greater rise for concern if used by an adult. As Anna Freud points out, the use of *projection* too is quite natural for very young children. Desires to do forbidden acts may be projected on to pets or dolls and they may be criticized and chastised accordingly. Where fixation has occurred at an early stage of development or where a particular mechanism has been habitually resorted to, this may become the characteristic way in which the adult learns to reduce anxiety. In part, personality emerges from the typical defences we come to employ. Note though that such defences operate normally on an unconscious level. Ego processes should by no means be regarded as synonymous with consciousness.

Ego psychology then offers a set of concepts which help us to distinguish the processes whereby individuals cope with conflict, both within themselves and between themselves and aspects of the outside world. It reveals to us the multiple determinants of our actions and the potential complexity of the motivational forces governing behaviour. Outward shows if not 'least themselves' are not necessarily what they seem. Vehement proclamation of love or loyalty *may* mask the very opposite. A child's aggressiveness *may*, in fact, be the product of fear. Intensive concern about the dangers of pornography *may* be fuelled by repressed libidinal needs, aroused into uncomfortable conflict by too direct exposure to that which they seek to express. Refusal to compete with others or engage in a constructive activity *may* be a defence against the possibility of realizing or reawakening feelings of inferiority. Even altruism *may* result from a combination of identification and projection of hopes and desires on to others. By gratifying them, the altruistic person is thus able to gratify himself.

CHAPTER 6

Theory of Neurosis

Before leaving this exposition of Freud's ideas, I would like to consider briefly his theory of neurosis and the practice of psychoanalysis as therapy. In a sense, the former at least has already been covered in the preceding sections. As Freud put it 'The theory of neuroses is psychoanalysis itself'.[1] All the ingredients for understanding Freud's view of neurosis have been presented in considering his idea of a dynamic unconscious, his theory of psychosexual development and the operation of defence mechanisms. Freud, in effect, draws no strict dividing line between normals and neurotics. It is a difference of degree rather than kind. He considered as one of his chief findings that:

> The neuroses (unlike infectious diseases, for instance) have no specific determinants. It would be idle to seek in them for pathogenic excitants. They shade off by easy transitions into what is described as the normal; and, on the other hand, there is scarcely any state recognized as normal in which indications of neurotic traits could not be pointed out.[2]

The fact that the illustrative examples I have used represent a mixture of case studies of patients and examples taken from everyday life reinforces this point.

Freud began his career as a scientist and, although much of his mature life was spent doing therapy, he still remained at heart a seeker after understanding. The great advantage to him of analysing patients rather than normals was that, in them, the processes of psychological functioning were thrown into greater relief.

Freud's focus of concern was what he called the *psychoneuroses*. He distinguished these from the *actual neuroses* which he somewhat vaguely conceived of as being due to the physiological effects of either an excess or frustration of sexual activity. The origin of psychoneuroses, on the other hand, were essentially of a deeper, psychological nature.

It was Freud's exploration of one kind of psychoneurosis – *hysteria* – which provided the foundation stone of his theory. *Conversion hysteria* (now rarely seen) expresses itself in physical symptoms, like the leg pains of Elizabeth von R. discussed on p. 48. *Anxiety hysteria* typically takes the form of a phobic reaction and is illustrated by Bertha Pappenheim's refusal to drink (see p. 27).

Equally, if not more important for psychoanalysis, was Freud's later exploration of *obsessional neurosis*. This condition is characterized by obsessional thoughts and compulsive behaviours often of a stereotyped, ritualized kind which, if not followed through precisely, result in a great deal of anxiety. So one of his patients[3] would insist on a complicated ritual each night before involved removal of all clocks, watches and vases, as well as a particular arrangement of pillows and eiderdown. A classic example of obsessional neurosis is Freud's study of Lorenz, often called the 'rat man' because of his obsessive fantasy about his father and girlfriend in which a pot of rats was fastened to their buttocks to gnaw into the anus.

> The chief features of his disorder were *fears* that something might happen to two people of whom he was very fond – his father and the lady whom he admired. Besides this he was aware of *compulsive impulses* – such as an impulse, for instance, to cut his throat with a razor; and further he produced *prohibitions*, sometimes in connection with quite unimportant things. He had wasted years, he told me, in fighting against these ideas of his . . .[4]

As the illustrations earlier in this chapter have made clear, Freud believed that the source of neurotic symptoms lies in unconscious conflict and the blocking or imbalance of energy flow which such conflict creates. The symptoms very often represent a symbolic defence against an unacceptable wish. But they do not serve just to block the desire. Like parapraxes and dreams, they also indirectly express the conflict, though in a way of which the patient is usually unaware. For example, the frustrated desire of Freud's patient Elizabeth von R. for her brother-in-law was associated with a walk in the woods with him. Her symptoms included leg pains which made it difficult for her to walk. The skill of the analyst is to trace the meaning of the symptoms. As with dreams, this is complicated by the fact that they are often *over-determined*. Several underlying conflicts may be woven into the fabric of a patient's symptoms. Elizabeth's leg pains, Freud believed, were also related to the actions involved in caring for her father, another situation which had required her to repress her own need.

Although symptoms are likely to be troublesome, it must be remembered that they are, nevertheless, *adaptive* – a way of adjusting to an intolerable situation. They are likely to offer some gain. The suffering they impose may help to assuage the patient's guilt; their disabling nature may help him to avoid future situations likely to generate conflict.

For Freud, the conflicts which underlie neuroses have an essentially sexual basis. As he expressed it in his final work, 'The symptoms of neuroses are . . . without exception a substitute satisfaction of some sexual urge or measures to prevent such a satisfaction; and as a rule they are compromises between the two.'⁵ With practically all his patients, he found the analytic trail led eventually to a repressed conflict centred on some kind of sexual experience as a child. But how did the different forms of neuroses arise? Freud's thinking on this matter underwent change. At first, he attributed them to the different nature of the 'seductions' which he assumed to have taken place when his patients had been children. The hysterics he considered had been passive partners, whereas the obsessional neurotics had taken a more active, interested role. As he put it in a letter to his friend Fliess, 'Hysteria is the consequence of a presexual *sexual shock*. Obsessional neurosis is the consequence of presexual *sexual pleasure* later transformed into guilt.'⁶

He later accepted that this seduction theory was an error. Such a prevalence of adult abuse seemed unlikely even given the 'nurse maids, governesses and domestic servants' whom he held primarily responsible. His own self-analysis stimulated his growing awareness of the power of children's fantasies. By the time of the *Three Essays on the Theory of Sexuality* he had revised his hypothesis. He now realized that the underlying conflict in his patients was created by their own feelings rather than by being seduced. He argued, as we have seen, that their source lay in the vicissitudes of psychosexual development in the first five years of life. He regarded the Oedipal conflict as the nucleus of all psychoneuroses. It generates the need to repress desire and lays down a basis of guilt and anxiety over the consequences of illicit longings. If inadequately resolved, it can undermine later capacity to form effective relationships with both sexes.

The different kinds of neuroses arise because of somewhat different patterns of regression and fixation. At the phallic stage repression is the primary mode of defence. Repression is not possible until fairly late on in development when a sense of differentiation between self and outside world ('object relations') has been achieved. The hysteric's reasonably good capacity for relating to other people also suggests regression to a later stage of development and makes prognosis good. The characteristic pattern of symptoms shown by the obsessional, on the other hand – stubborn adherence to ritual and a rigid, often excessively fastidious and orderly style – is strongly reminiscent of the anal phase. Their critical and aggressive feelings and the obsessive detail with which they recount experiences makes analysis more problematic.

In his later writings, Freud came to emphasize more the role of anxiety in neurosis. At first, he had seen anxiety as representing a transmutation of blocked libido. Then he began to view it as expressing fear of loss – particularly of the mother (separation anxiety) and the penis (castration anxiety). The prototype for this is the birth trauma where the baby is painfully expelled from the warmth and security of his mother's womb. One of Freud's followers, Otto Rank,[7] developed this as the core of his own theory, for him displacing even psychosexual development in its significance.

In Freud's later theory, as we have seen, anxiety comes to be regarded as arising primarily from conflict between the varied demands made upon the ego in its task of balancing the satisfaction of instinctual needs against the moral constraints of the superego and the realistic consequences likely to be entailed in the outside world. The different forms of psychoneurosis can be conceptualized in terms of the defence mechanisms they primarily employ – isolation and undoing, for example, in obsessional neurosis, and repression and sometimes displacement (i.e., of repressed libido into physical symptoms) in the case of hysteria. (Hysteria may also involve *dissociation* where, because of repression, different aspects of personality exist relatively independently – the rare and extreme cases being 'split' personalities of the Jekyll and Hyde and the 'Three Faces of Eve' type).[8] This conceptualization is, of course, quite consistent with the earlier idea of regression and fixation. The defensive process prominent at the stage of development where fixation occurs characterizes the form that the later neurotic symptoms will take. But it does tend to emphasize the significance of the ego in both psychological health and in therapy – an idea which has been stressed and amplified by later analysts in the Freudian tradition.

Freud considered that anxiety, conflict and repression are intrinsic features of civilized life. No one can avoid the trauma of birth. Socialization inevitably involves some frustration of our desires and their fulfilment. The process of development involves finding a way to express our needs in the face of an often unsatisfactory reality. Most of us learn to cope in some way though we may well bear the scars that anxiety and frustration inflict. The neurotics among us, because of the force of their early needs and/or the nature of their childhood relationships, have borne more than their share. All that distinguishes them (and a blurred boundary it is) is that they did not find ways of coping that were effective enough.

By no means all psychological disorders are open to treatment by psychoanalysis. And we shall see, one of the basic features of psychoanalytic therapy is the analysis of transference. Freud believed that during analysis the patient is likely to transfer his feelings, including those from early childhood which are at the root of his conflict, on to his analyst. It is by working through these feelings that both insights and change come about. The psychoneuroses discussed above are open to this kind of approach, which is why they are often called 'transference neuroses'. But the traumatic neuroses which Freud encountered during the First World War are unamenable to such a method, for they do not arise from conflicting desires but from a specific and overwhelming experience of shock. The symptoms (e.g., nightmares, anxiety attacks) do not represent so much a way of resolving unconscious conflict but rather, Freud believed, they symbolize repetitions of the shock episode as part of the patient's attempts to gain control or mastery over it.

Another cardinal requirement for effective psychoanalysis is that the patient, on a surface level at least, should *want* to change. This tends to place the so-called 'behaviour disorders' outside the analyst's reach. For here the presenting problem is the difficulty that the person gets himself or others into rather than any personal experience of distress. An example of this kind is the psychopathic personality. His or her primary characteristic is absence of moral scruple and of capacity for any real emotional involvement with others. On the surface he may appear charming and intelligent. But he acts on the slightest whim and with little regard to the consequences for himself or the welfare of others. There may be later apologies for his actions but rarely evidence of remorse. He can on occasion be violent though more often he becomes a persistent petty criminal. In psychoanalytic terms, such a pattern indicates a failure of superego development – that, as a child, he was unable to identify sufficiently with an adult to develop through internalization his own system of inner principles and controls. Psychologically he is a young child in adult clothing.

Most intractable of all are the *psychoses*. This term embraces a group of disorders (such as schizophrenia and intense depression) whose common characteristic is defective 'reality testing' – an inability to see the world as others see it. In extreme form, this may involve hallucinations or delusions. Although Freud does not deny that physiological factors may be operative in psychoses, in psychoanalytic terms the critical problem is a profound failure of ego functioning. Psychosis represents, in effect, a deep regression to an early stage of development (such as the oral stage) before the ego had adequately formed. Such a person is incapable of cathecting or investing libido in other people and the outside world. Instead, it is turned back on the self. In Freud's terms, these are *narcissistic* disorders. The psychotic withdraws to live in his own inner world of fantasy – in a state of intense self-absorption. Because of the extreme difficulty of establishing a therapeutic relationship, Freud considered (though other analysts have not always agreed with him) that psychoanalysis was useless in such cases and, indeed, may even exacerbate the condition.

CHAPTER 7

The Practice of Analysis as Therapy

In this account of psychoanalysis so far, I have focused largely on its *theory* and made relatively little mention of its techniques for *therapy*. It is important to distinguish between the two. They clearly go hand in hand. Freud's theory evolved out of careful observation of his patients and, in turn, influenced the therapeutic procedures he adopted. But reading Freud's clinical studies, it is hard to avoid the suspicion that 'curing' patients was subsidiary to his interest in therapeutic work as a source and testing ground for his ideas.

Freud's method of therapy was developed and modified over the span of his career. Initially it was essentially *abreactive* – that is, its main aim was to encourage patints to recollect and to express the repressed and forgotten traumatic emotions responsible, as Freud believed, for their symptoms. This act of emotional catharsis constituted the cure. Later, the emphasis shifted to gauging the underlying meaning of a patient's condition and conveying this interpretation to him. The aim was to enlighten the patient about his repressions and characteristic defences; to encourage him to become aware of unconscious, irrational mechanisms and to replace them with rational decisions. 'We tried to restore the ego, to free it from its restrictions, and to give it back the command over the id which it has lost owing to its early repressions.'[1]

Acceptance by the patient of the analyst's interpretation is never though just a cognitive exercise. It is important that he experiences the desires and conflicts concerned and not just knows about them. By re-experiencing them and repeatedly working them through in this way, the patient learns to integrate them within his conscious ego functioning. They come under his control.

In pursuit of these ends, Freud tried out and developed a range of techniques. As noted earlier, he experimented with hypnosis to aid patients' recall of repressed events but soon discarded it. With many patients, it was not possible to produce a sufficient depth of trance and, even when it was, patients had great difficulties in fully accepting and integrating interpretations gleaned in this way. Freud next developed his 'concentration' technique. This was based on a method used by Bernheim (one of the clinicians whom Freud had visited early in his career) to induce his subject to remember what earlier, when hypnotized, they had been instructed to forget. It consisted of pressing his hand on his patient's forehead and assuring him that, when the pressure was relaxed, the memory would return. Freud found this concentration technique as effective as hypnosis for aiding patients' recall. Gradually he developed the armoury of methods for penetrating unconscious meaning which we have already considered – free association and the interpretations of patients' dreams, parapraxes and everyday actions.

Patients are quite often, of course, reluctant to accept the interpretation they are offered. Such 'resistance' is seen by the therapist as further material for analysis to be worked through accordingly. This may provide in particular insights into the defensive stratagems used by the patient.

As suggested in the previous section, the most important procedure for Freud was the analysis of *transference*. He observed that, during the course of therapy, the patient seems to transfer onto the analyst his feelings towards his parents and other significant people in his life, particularly when these had been a source of emotional conflict in the past. The relationship between patient and therapist thus becomes an important source of information. It can be analysed and worked through to yield understanding of the patient's early emotional ties. In the early phases of analysis, transference typically goes through a positive phase. The patient expresses great admiration for his analyst and may become emotionally attached to him to the point of jealousy. This is followed by a negative phase (especially when both are male) where the patient is likely to become aggressive and critical. These positive and negative phases reflect, Freud believed, a working through of the ambivalence experienced in the child's relationships with his parents.

Transference does not occur solely on the patient's side. The treatment by Freud's colleague Breuer of Bertha Pappenheim was described earlier. Pollock[2] suggests that the reason why Breuer seemed to become so disturbed and suddenly broke off his analysis with the girl might have been a problem of counter-transference. There were certainly similarities in their experience which may well have complicated Breuer's feelings for his patient. During the course of her therapy, Bertha's father had died. She had cared for him devotedly while he was ill and her intense grief at his death lead to several suicide attempts. These feelings had been a significant theme explored in her analysis. Breuer's own mother (who was also called Bertha) had died when he was only three. His father had raised and tutored him and they became very close. Like Bertha, Breuer had suffered profound distress when his own father had subsequently died.

Analysts are human too which is one reason why analysis of the analyst is such an important part of his training. This, together with the consciously adopted stance of neutrality, is his supposed armour against entanglement in the complications of counter-transference.

CHAPTER 8

Freud's Progeny — Developments in Psychoanalysis

One of Freud's greatest achievements was his capacity to stimulate the creativity of others. Psychoanalysis did not stand still. Freud's ideas have been developed by his followers in a bewildering variety of ways. Before going on to examine the nature of psychoanalysis in Part Two, this chapter offers a broad review of some of the main strands in the evolution of psychoanalytic thought.

Black Sheep

As early as the first years of this century, Freud's writings began to attract a band of followers interested in his ideas. He was especially gratified by the interest of one of three visitors from Zurich he received in 1907. This was Carl Jung, a Swiss psychiatrist from the well-known Burghölzli Clinic, with whom he had been corresponding for some time. Not only was Freud flattered by the attentions of an established psychologist but he was impressed by his visitor's vitality and imagination. In 1910, when the International Psychoanalytic Society was formed, much to Freud's approval Jung became its first president. By that time a small group of loyal disciples had formed round Freud including Max Eitington, Alfred Adler, Karl Abraham and Otto Rank, Sandor Ferenczi from Hungary and Ernest Jones, later Freud's biographer, from Britain. Both Jung and Ferenczi accompanied Freud in the following year on his visit to America for the Clark University lectures. But soon after the inception of the International Society, rifts began to develop. In part these were due to personal jealousies. Adler and other Viennese analysts, for example, resented the prominence of the Swiss contingent. But it was difficult for a member of the group to develop an original theme of his own without incurring Freud's displeasure. He did not welcome radical departures from his ideas. The only way to do this was to break away.

Adler was the first to go in 1911. Ostensibly he disagreed with Freud's emphasis on sexuality as the primary force motivating human behaviour. He wanted to emphasize, in its place, the drive for power or 'striving for superiority' in compensation for feelings of inferiority. He regarded the latter as an inevitable part of being human. They have their roots in the helplessness experienced as a child. Early on in an individual's life, he or she develops ways of compensating for inferiority feelings. This forms the basis of character and later 'life-style', which will be reflected in the adult's way of coping with the problem areas of life – work, love and social relationships. Successful strategies in the search for personal esteem require courage and the ability to confront reality. Problems arise when a person overcompensates for inadequacy by unrealistically grandiose behaviour or conceptions of himself. Overwhelming need for personal esteem can also create problems in relationships. Power over another may become of greater interest than gratification. Frigidity, for example, may be a way of asserting superiority over a partner.

Adler stressed the importance of relationships in early childhood. The position of a child relative to his siblings assumes considerable significance. The first-born, for example, is the 'dethroned king'. Having once had the exclusive attention of his parents, he is displaced by the arrival of his younger siblings. More responsibility tends to be thrust upon him and he usually retains the edge of ability and power over his younger rivals. Such conditions set the scene for the development of his life-style. In contrast, the second child has to strive to compete. The youngest never has to confront being displaced in the affections of his family. But he is aware of the greater ability and power of the others. Adler points out that in fairy stories it is often the youngest son who is favoured by fortune and is able to succeed even when his more able older brothers have failed. Adler also attributes significance to the attitude of parents towards their children: whether, to take two extremes, they spoil or hate them.

Adler emphasized the wholeness of the patient and in his 'individual' psychotherapy was concerned to work through the patient's conscious awareness of his strivings and life situation as well as unconscious desires. He tended to place less emphasis than Freud on the biological basis of emotional development. This is instanced, for example, in his notion of 'masculine protest'. Many of the significant features of feminine character development arise not from awareness of anatomical differences as in Freud's theory but because of the social pressures on girls created by conventional social roles. 'Masculine protest' represents the reaction of some girls to the inferior status thrust upon them, by rejecting their own sex and by over-assertion of male characteristics – in other words by becoming a tomboy.

Adler was an energetic speaker and a readable writer. Even though his ideas do not easily form into a coherent theory, his approach and work have had considerable influence on both other analysts and the lay public. It is perhaps not surprising that Adler's ideas would have general appeal as their focus on conscious processes fits in more easily with commonsense notions of the self. A greater emphasis on consciousness and the analysis of ego processes though is characteristic of the therapy of many post-Freudian analysts and the seeds he had sown of interest in social forces on the personality of women were later taken up and developed by Karen Horney.

Adler's apostasy led to Freud publicly criticizing him in his lectures. What was new in Adler's theory, he argued, was trivial. The rest was merely a version of his own ideas. The quarrel split the newly-formed society and several members left along with Adler. But much more powerful for Freud was the worsening of relations between himself and *Jung*. Eventually they parted in 1913 and never met again. Like Adler, Jung disagreed with Freud's focus on the importance of sexuality. Jung's 'libido' was conceived as a more general 'life energy' of which sex was only one of the main forms. Later, Freud himself moved closer to this position when, in *Beyond the Pleasure Principle*,[1] he reformulated his theory of instincts, grouping both sexual instincts (concerned with preservation of species) and ego instincts (concerned with preservation of self) together as the life drives or *Eros* – a point often unacknowledged by Jungians. Jung also modified Freud's developmental theory, seeing, rather like Adler, the child's total relationships with his parents as significant for later characteristics rather than just focusing on psychosexual development. Regression was not regarded necessarily as negative. Often it could be a useful device whereby an individual could temporarily withdraw from conflict in order to cope better later.

Imagination for Jung, unlike lucidity, was never in short supply and he developed a host of new concepts. He introduced the term 'complex', for example, to refer to a cluster of feelings related to a significant aspect of a person's world, and devised the word association test where length of time responding or the kind of associations given to certain words are used as clues to uncover them. He originated a theory of personality types based on the notions of introversion and extraversion and different ways of apprehending the world (intuition versus sensation) and evaluating it (reason versus feeling). Although Jung began, with his word association test, by trying to find a more scientific basis for psychoanalysis, his later writings are often obscure and mystical and some of his ideas have aroused considerable controversy. Jung was impressed with the parallels he found between the symbols found in the myths and art of widely disparate cultures and noted that they sometimes resembled the paintings and the dream images recalled by his patients. He postulated a 'collective unconscious' as the foundation of mental life. He considered this deepest stratum of the unconscious to represent a residue of experiences acquired by modern man's remote ancestors. The symbols arising from the collective unconscious Jung called _archetypes_ and they are considered to represent in distilled form central universal experiences in human life. Although Jung claimed that archetypes exist only as predispositions to respond to certain images, his notion of the collective unconscious does seem to imply a controversial Lamarckian view of inheritance – that characteristics acquired in the course of life can be transmitted genetically.

Jung's therapeutic approach has been as innovative as his theory. He focused on the significance of meaning in a patient's life. How does he make sense of his own personal existence? What gives point and purpose to it? His interest was more in the present and the future – what the patient is and will become – rather than his childhood past. Jung's approach was philosophical and in his writings he has delved into issues of morality and religion, which he believed are inseparable from the mental life of human beings. He is more prepared than Freud to accept explicitly the essentially moral nature of mental life, a position argued for later in this book. Jung's therapeutic approach was flexible, designed to suit the needs of individual patients. His theory and therapy both emphasized the notion of balance. The more an aspect of personality is emphasized in conscious active life, the more the need grows to express its opposite characteristic in the unconscious. The particular method he developed – _individuation_ – focused on getting the patient to face the deep, inner forces of his unconscious and, by integrating these into awareness, develop more fully his potential self. It is a procedure suited to older patients and often has considerable appeal to creative people concerned to develop their inner resources.

The possibility that psychoanalysis may be 'biased' by its dependence on introspection and self-analysis has already been discussed. It is interesting to note, in view of the differing emphases of their theories, that Adler was short, Jewish and, by contemporary accounts, ambitious but suffered pronounced inferiority feelings.[2] Jung, whose work not only reveals a distaste for Freud's emphasis on sex but a ponderous, Germanic erudition and a love of mysticism, was the son of a minister of the Swiss

Reformed Church, and a teetotaller. The variations they felt impelled to introduce, as well as the conflict between them and Freud, seem due as much to incompatibility of personality and background as rational dissent.

Somewhat later, in the 1920s, came the secessions of Rank and Reich. *Otto Rank* had been a key figure in Freud's early circle. He had no medical training but was a well-educated and cultured man and Freud recognized his great ability. The book which eventually led to the split between them, in fact represented an extension of one of Freud's own ideas. He had observed that the physiological symptoms of anxiety resembled the physical changes which occur during the process of birth. Rank took up the notion of *birth trauma* as the core of human experience. It provides the prototype of an antithesis between union and separateness which is echoed at different points through life. On one hand is the *life fear* – that self-assertion may lead to separation from security and all that is good. On the other, is the *death fear* – that union will lead to loss of individuality and freedom.

Rank reinterpreted the psychoanalytic theory of human development in this light. Weaning becomes a problem of separation from the mother. Genitality becomes a symbolic opportunity for the male to re-enter the mother by sexual penetration. The Oedipus conflict becomes displaced as the nuclear issue in the development of personality. Aggression becomes a mode of assertion of individuality. By fighting her parents an adolescent, for example, can assert a sense of self. A key concept in Rank's later theory was the notion of *will*. Will is the integrative, assertive force of personality. Through will and counterwill (the ability to say no to oneself and others) a balance can be developed between the needs to belong and to be free. At the core of neurosis is the failure to achieve this integration. In his therapy, Rank was very concerned not to encourage passivity and dependence. To this end he experimented with brief therapy, setting a definite limit to the number of sessions it would involve.

There has been some resurgence of Rank's ideas outside the psychoanalytic fold. They have been applied in a dramatic form in the recent vogue for 'rebirthing'. In a darkened room and often with the support of taped sounds of a heart beating and circulating fluids, an attempt is made to recreate the experience of birth. This may involve hyperventilation (i.e., rapid heavy breathing) or the application of womb-like pressure from a press of other bodies. Reliving the experience, advocates of this method believe, helps exorcize the trauma of original birth.

The subsequent career of another apostate of this time, *Wilhelm Reich*, was colourful indeed. He met Freud in 1919, was excited by both him and pychoanalysis and quickly became an energetic member of the Vienna group. Although highly original, his thinking was often rather simplistic. He had a rather grandiose opinion of himself which often made it difficult for him to get on with people. He broke off training with different analysts no fewer than three times and suffered chagrin when Freud refused to take him on. After a few years he left the group for Berlin. He became excited by Communism but got on with his political comrades no better. He moved from Berlin to Scandinavia, eventually settling in Oslo. Wherever he went, he attracted loyal followers and bitter critics.

The initial ideas of Reich which had increasingly alienated him from Freud and more orthodox psychoanalysts, were centred on the problem of free expression of sexuality. He was interested in the influence of society on character but particularly in the effects of the constraints it imposes on libidinal needs. (This antagonism between social pressure and instinct is not unlike Freud's view, particularly as he expressed it in a book published late in his career (1930) *Civilisation and its Discontents*).[3] The most acceptable aspect of Reich's ideas for other analysts has been his notion of 'character armour'. This is that continuous blocking of energy due to anxiety, especially in childhood, can lead to muscular tensions of a relatively permanent kind. Reich believed that sexual orgasm served a vital function as the most important mode of release for blocked energy. The search for ways of measuring and creating life energy preoccupied him in his increasingly unsettled and undisciplined final years. He devised an 'orgone box' which he claimed would accumulate bio-energy and would benefit a person, or indeed any organism, sitting inside – he even claimed it as a partial cure for cancer and that he could control the weather, making rain by pointing orgone accumulator tubes at clouds to increase their vapour content. Unlike standard analytic practice, in his therapy he involved himself directly with his patients. The basic problem as he saw it was to get blocked energy flowing again. A key approach was to help them towards a greater capacity for sexual expression. He would encourage them to masturbate, use massage to break down body armour and was reported as having sexual relations with some of his patients.

Reich was eventually refused permission to stay in both Sweden and Norway because of what was regarded as the flagrancy of his published ideas. He settled in the USA and in the 1940s and 1950s became quite prosperous from his salary as an Associate Professor in New York and then from therapy, books and the sale of the orgone accumulators which he had devised. He ran foul of the US Food and Drink Administration who objected to him shipping over state lines a device which purported to be a cure for cancer. Reich's paranoid grandiosity led him to refute the legitimacy of the charges. His mishandling of the case and refusal to obey the court's ruling resulted in a two-year prison sentence. After a few months spent fairly comfortably in a 'country club' of a prison, he died of a heart attack in 1957. In spite of his often difficult ways, Reich attracted in his lifetime numerous followers and students. One of his great British admirers was A. S. Neill who started Summerhill, the first of the totally child-centred schools. He has left behind him a flourishing legacy – the bio-energetics movement active both in Europe and the USA. This focuses on the use of massage and physical exercises to try to stimulate energy flow and relieve blocks and tensions.

Child Analysis

Several developments of a less radical but nonetheless far-reaching kind have taken place in more recent years. In Britain, one emphasis has been to extend psychoanalysis to include work with children. Freud's youngest daughter Anna had accompanied him when he emigrated to London in the last year of his life. She had been his constant support, both personally and professionally, since her adolescent years. Contrary to normal analytic practice, he had analysed her himself. He referred to her as his 'faithful Antigone'. She was clearly devoted to her father and, Roazen[4] suggests, jealous of other women in his life. Anna had worked as a school teacher. It was this and perhaps her own role in relation to her father that drew her interest to developing techniques for the analysis of children. Her approach was orthodox but she found that she needed to introduce variations because of the difference between children and adults. She worked only with children who were old enough to express themselves and give her some co-operation. Her first task was to engage their interest and to convince them of her potential value to them. She used the interpretation of dreams and fantasy and a form of transference analysis – though with children the relationship with the therapist could be regarded only as an extension rather than a re-enactment of feelings for their parents. A particular innovation she later introduced is the 'metapsychological profile'. This is designed to assist an analyst in systematically getting together all the relevant information about a child during the period of diagnostic assessment. It is, like Anna Freud's own approach, essentially integrative. It requires taking into account the pattern of instinctual expression, development and the mechanisms of defence adopted to cope with conflict. After settling in England, she set up the Hampstead Clinic and Nurseries where she treated both British and later German orphans of the Second World War as well as other children.

Child analysis was already established in London well before the arrival of Anna Freud and her father. *Melanie Klein* had been analysing children in Berlin since the 1920s and emigrated to London in 1926. Like Anna Freud she had no formal academic or scientific training, but her approach was very different. They had clashed in their ideas at a psycho-analytic conference as early as 1927. The critical difference between them revolved round Klein's revision of developmental theory. Essentially she saw everything as occurring much earlier than Freud supposed. The most critical phases come in the first year of life. During that time, she believed, even Oedipal conflict can be experienced and the vestiges of ego and superego functioning are already apparent. The infant's primitive differentiation of self and world leads him to project his feelings on to the key objects in his world. These take on both negative and positive qualities (e.g., the 'good' and 'bad' breast) depending on their often dual role in frustrating and gratifying at different times. Klein's focus is not so much on sexuality as on the child's handling of aggression and rage induced by frustration.

The task of analysis is to help reduce the anxiety the child inevitably feels and so to reduce aggressiveness. Klein was prepared to take on children below the age of 6 and she used their play as both a diagnostic and therapeutic medium. As fear and rage are necessary concomitants of development, Klein has advocated analysis for all children. Again Anna Freud demurs, believing it is only appropriate for those who have shown specific personality or behavioural problems. Freud himself is reported to have found Klein's ideas 'unintelligible' and she has been criticized by orthodox analysts for assuming far too great a complexity in the emotional life of the year-old infant. But her ideas have brought her a considerable British following and helped lead to the development of the influential 'object relations' group.

Yet another difference between Klein and Anna Freud is the former's emphasis on the development of biological drives. As we saw in Chapter 5, apart from her work with children, Anna Freud's main theoretical contribution was to extend her father's embryonic ideas of the significance of the ego and mechanisms of defence. Several other analysts, in particular Hartmann,[5] have taken this lead with a greater emphasis on more detailed analyis of ego functions.

Neo-Freudians

Many analysts left Nazi-dominated central Europe to settle in the USA. Among those who did so were Erich Fromm, Karen Horney and Erik Erikson. In their elaboration of psychoanalytic theory, we again sense the significance of personal context. All three had direct experience of a society in the process of becoming totalitarian. All three had to break the pattern of their lives and to start anew in an alien culture. They could thus compare the patients and the problems characteristically found in the two societies. Not surprisingly, all three place much more stress than Freud did on the significance of cultural context. Horney specifically rejects what she regards as Freud's over-emphasis on biological determinants, particularly in regard to the differential early development of the sexes. Both Fromm and Horney had been influenced by Marxist theory.

Fromm differs from both Freud and Reich in his view of the nature of the relationship between the individual and society. For him it is not necessarily an antithetical one. It is not a question of the needs of the individual existing relatively independently of society and tending to be frustrated by social constraints. Rather, society provides the medium through which an individual can attain satisfactions and helps to determine the form his needs will take. The relation between the individual and society is not static but will vary according to historical period and culture. It is essentially interactive. Society provides the conditions through which an individual learns to satisfy his needs. But the individual's needs shaped in this way in turn have the potential to influence and to change the nature of the society in which he lives. The key issue for individuals is how they *relate* to others and the world around them.

Fromm's approach has not only a Marxist but also a strong existentialist core. He is interested in the problems that arise from the central characteristic of being human – the high level of capacity for symbolic thought which permits *self-awareness*.

> Man is the only animal who not only knows objects but who knows that he knows. Man is the only animal who has not only instrumental intelligence, but reason, the capacity to use his thinking to understand objectively – i.e. to know the nature of things as they are in themselves, and not only as means for his satisfaction. Gifted with self-awareness and reason, man is aware of himself as a being separate from nature and from others; he is aware of his powerlessness, of his ignorance, he is aware of his end: death.⁶

Freud provided a very useful, if sometimes confusing, foundation for relating the biological and existential aspects of man. Fromm takes this further by postulating a fundamental contradiction between human biological roots and capacity for self-awareness.

> Self-awareness, reason and imagination have disrupted the 'harmony' that characterizes animal existence. Their emergence has made man into an anomaly, the freak of the universe. He is part of nature, subject to her physical laws and unable to change them, yet he transcends nature. He is set apart while being a part; he is homeless, yet chained to the home he shares with all creatures. Cast into this world at an accidental place and time he is forced out of it accidentally and against his will. Being aware of himself, he realises his powerlessness and the limitations of his existence. He is never free from the dichotomy of his existence: he cannot rid himself of his mind, even if he would want to; he cannot rid himself of his body as long as he is alive – and his body makes him want to be alive.[7]

This contradiction gives rise to what he calls 'existential dichotomies'. One is the need to confront the fact of our own eventual death. While we know that we are alive now, we know also that we are creatures imprisoned within a finite life span – that one day we will die. We are confronted too by the need for choice. We are aware that what we choose to do now can influence what happens and what we will be in the future.

As a child grows so he or she will gradually become aware of a sense of intrinsic separateness. Such *individuation* (note that Fromm uses this term very differently from Jung) is probably unique to the human species. People find different ways of relating to others to overcome this sense of isolation. Fromm suggests that conformity is a prevalent solution:

> . . . a union in which the individual self disappears to a large extent, and where the aim is to belong to the herd. If I am like everybody else, if I have no feelings or thoughts which make me different, if I conform in custom, dress, to the pattern of the group, I am saved; saved from the frightening experience of aloneness.[8]

Another and much more satisfactory way of relating, Fromm argues, is through love. He defines this word, though, in a rather special way to mean 'union under the condition of preserving one's integrity, one's individuality . . . love makes (man) overcome the sense of isolation and separateness, yet it permits him to be himself, to retain his integrity'.[9]

Fromm has extended Freud's theory of psychosexual development to emphasize the different ways of relating that are possible. That emerging from the oral stage, for example, is a passive, *receptive* one. Everything which is good is outside the person and there is an overwhelming desire to absorb from the outside. Another character type which Fromm delineates is the *exploitative* type whose mode of relating is aggressive, taking what he needs by force. The *hoarding* character, in anal style, is concerned with retaining what he already has. His relations with the outside world are withdrawn and suspicious. The *marketing* character relates to others as a commercial transaction. He tends to appreciate himself and other things only in terms of their value to others. Finally, Fromm's *productive* character is a blend of Marxist and existentialist ideals. He relates to the world through productive work and creativity, his relationships are characterized by love as defined above and he accepts the need to make authentic choices and 'to realize the powers inherent in him'.

In more recent writings, Fromm has expressed styles of relating as a polarity of oppositional modes. One formulation[10] of this is the contrast between 'biophiles' and 'necrophiles'. The former are fundamentally concerned with life and growth. The latter view life in negative terms – 'people are rotten'. There is a preoccupation with that which is decayed and dead, often revealing itself in a fascination for the mechanical. When listening to music, for example, it is likely to be the quality of the stero that interests them; when taking photos the gadgetry of the camera. Another formulation[11] is the distinction between *having* and *being*. In the first case, life is measured in terms of possessions – of objects, wealth and status. In the other, it is gauged in terms of quality of experience and awareness.

Fromm emphasizes though, as we have seen, that individuals do not exist in a vacuum. The social contexts in which they live serve to encourage certain styles of relating rather than others. Each culture has a kind of 'social unconscious'. Its members are influenced not only by explicit prohibitions but by what is encouraged as normal and reasonable behaviour and the shared conventions of speech and thought.

Like Jung, Fromm's emphasis in therapy is on the search for meaning and finding a satisfactory style of relating to others and the world. But this cannot be satisfactorily achieved by simply conforming to the meanings offered by society and others. It is an inevitably personal search. Fromm's humanistic conclusion is that 'there is no meaning to life except the meaning man gives his life by the unfolding of his powers'.[12]

Even in her early papers published in German, *Karen Horney* had criticized Freud's biological emphasis, particularly his view of the psychical consequences of anatomical characteristics in the development of girls. After emigrating to the USA in 1932 she set about developing her ideas, eventually publishing five books and founding a breakaway psychoanalytic movement. Adler's influence is apparent on her work and she has expressed considerable admiration for the writings of Erich Fromm. In her interest in the notion of self-development and her optimistic belief in the capacity of people for growth once the obstacles of neurotic inhibitions have been overcome, she anticipated the approach of Carl Rogers and other humanistic psychologists.

The key characteristics of her approach are best illuminated by comparison with Freudian theory. Like Freud, she accepts that the patient's symptoms are determined by unconscious emotional feelings. In her conceptualization of the neurotic personality she acknowledges the influence of childhood experience and the operation of defensive processes. Her primary point of departure is that, while she accepts that constitutional factors may play some part in determining individual personality, she rejects Freud's emphasis on biological process and psychosexual drive. Such a position, she considers, takes insufficient account of more recent anthropological evidence as to the variability of human social life. She questions how far personality can be regarded as a universal phenomenon. Her experience of moving to the USA during the Depression reinforced this position. Her American patients seemed to her much more preoccupied with their work and financial prospects than sexual concerns. American society seemed to generate a different set of problems from those experienced by Freud's Viennese, middle-class patients. Horney came to consider that any neurosis has to be viewed against the context of the particular culture in which the individual lived. For her, the important source of neurotic conflict is interpersonal relations, particularly between a child and his parents. Thus the Oedipus complex is not universal nor does it specifically arise from sexual desires and inhibitions. It occurs as a result of a more general disturbance in family relations, when, for example, the child is made anxious by his parents' rejection. Sometimes Horney seems to stand Freudian ideas on their head. Thus sexual problems are more likely to be seen as originating in relationship difficulties rather than vice versa. She emphasizes too the influence of later life experience. Neurotic difficulties are no mere action replay of infantile conflicts but are transmuted and influenced by contemporary circumstances.

The focus of Horney's writings is on the nature of the 'neurotic personality'. She sees the roots of neurosis as lying in the child's early experience of his parents. Where this is negative – perhaps because of the parents' own neurotic difficulties – and fails to satisfy the child's needs for affection and approval, feelings of hostility are likely to be experienced by the child. But he may fear to express this because of the possibility of punishment or further withdrawal of love. Such an experience lays the foundation for what Horney sees as the core of neurotic personality disturbance – *'basic anxiety'*. Neurotic trends consist of the strategies which are developed to assuage such anxiety when coping with people and life situations. Horney has delineated ten such strategies but has further grouped these under three broad orientations. One general way of coping is to '*move towards people*' – for example, by indiscriminately seeking their affection and approval, or by trying to find a partner as a protector, or by giving way to others and restricting one's own demands so as not to conflict with them. A second general strategy is to '*move against people*'. The threat of others is removed by seeking power over them and getting the better of them. This pattern may involve a craving for prestige and the admiration of others, or concern for perfection in order to ensure that one's own attainments are better than anyone else's. The third means of coping is withdrawal – '*to move away from people*'. This is an attempt to assuage anxiety by removing any need for dependency on other people by ensuring self-sufficiency and detachment.

Horney emphasizes that this three-fold scheme is not intended as a typology of different forms of neurosis. More than one type of strategy may be utilized by the same individual on different occasions. They may even co-exist, creating a further source of inner conflict. It is from such conflicts that ' "neurotic symptoms" such as phobias, depressions, alcoholism, ultimately result.'[13]

The patterns she describes come within the canons of normal behaviour – most of us resort to one or other of them at different times as a way of coping with difficult situations. Why then should they be regarded as neurotic? Horney points out that they are distinguishable as neurotic trends when they 'are almost a caricature of the human values they resemble. They lack freedom, spontaneity and meaning . . . Their value . . . lies in the fact that they hold the more or less desperate promise of safety and of a solution for all problems.'[14] Such behaviours are revealed as neurotic by their compulsiveness and rigidity, the way they are applied almost regardless of situation.

Underlying the neurotic personality will be a disturbance in the way the self is experienced. Rather as Rogers was later to emphasize, Horney considered that the child, as a result of his basic anxiety, comes to regard his own self and feelings as despicable and valueless. Such self-rejection may be intensified by repressed hostility being turned against himself. A split develops between the negative way he experiences himself and the idealized self-image which is based on the admonitions and values of others, particularly the parents. This becomes the self he must attain to gain the affection and approval of others. But, as Horney points out, rather than serving as a stimulus to self-development, this becomes a hindrance. For it is an ideal which can never be achieved without the child denying what he feels himself to be.

She discusses the supplementary processes which neurotic persons may employ as further defences against anxiety and conflicts which have been created in these ways. One means is to *compartmentalize* different parts of life; another is to *blind themselves to the implications* of their actions where, for example, these conflict with the idealized self-image. Neurotic persons may seek refuge too in *elusiveness* – refusing to be pinned down or commit themselves; or they may justify their actions by *rationalization* or *cynicism*. One process which Horney considers to be particularly common is *externalization*. By this she means the tendency to attribute emotions and desires to other people. *Their* attitudes and actions become the focus of the neurotic person's life. He or she becomes 'preoccupied with changing them, reforming them, punishing them, protecting himself from their interference, or impressing them . . .'[15] Life becomes lived through others rather than himself.

For Horney, the goal of psychotherapy is to help patients gain the insight they require to change their neurotic strategies and express their potentials and capacity for growth. She tended to rely on most of the orthodox tools of psychoanalysis like free association and dream interpretation. But there was a fundamental difference in her attitude to the patient. She considered it quite justifiable to abandon the neutral stance of the orthodox analyst in order to give encouragement or sympathy to her patients whenever this seems called for. She regarded too the analysis of transference as a means of gaining insights into patients' current ways of relating to others as much as into their infantile relationships. In her book *Self-analysis*,[16] she also puts forward the view that even without the help of an analyst, it is possible to go quite a long way in working through resistances and analysing one's self.

What Horney's writings[17] offer are sensitive, descriptive accounts of the neurotic personality. If they find a ready response in the reader it is perhaps because she describes so well attitudes and behaviours that most of us have experienced in ourselves and others. However, her accounts are presented in a somewhat dogmatic, 'take-it-or-leave-it' fashion. Unlike other neo-Freudians and Freud himself, she rarely provides much in the way of supporting argument or substantive evidence for the assertions she makes. It is this which has lessened the impact she has had on the development of psychoanalysis. She presents not so much a psychological theory as a series of descriptive accounts of neurotic process.

After training as an artist and wandering about Europe for a while, *Erik Erikson* settled in Vienna to work as a teacher. There he was analysed by Anna Freud and eventually became a child analyst himself. Just before the Second World War he emigrated to the USA where he became an influential disseminator of psychoanalytic ideas. Erikson seeks to clarify and extend Freud's theory rather than to modify it in a fundamental way.

But the ingredients he adds significantly enrich psychoanalysis and enlarge its scope.

Like the other neo-Freudian *émigrés*, Erikson takes a particular interest in the influence of social context on personality. Shortly after his arrival in the States he went on two anthropological field trips to make studies of traditional patterns of child development in the Sioux and Yurok Indian tribes. His observations convinced him that personality is grounded in the cultural pattern of the society in which an individual is reared. This pattern is in turn related to the economic and geographical conditions on which the existence of that society depends. Thus the child-rearing methods of the Sioux foster a generous and courageous individuality appropriate to their tradition as a hunting and nomadic tribe of the Great Plains. The Yurok in contrast depend on ensnaring fish and live on the same sites as generations of ancestors before them. Their cultural pattern and child-rearing practices emphasize care, cleanliness and the acquisition of possessions. Erikson is not asserting a straightforward causal relationship between social context, child-rearing and individual personality, but rather that there is a 'mutual assimilation of somatic, mental and social patterns which amplify one another . . .'[18] He is arguing, however, that actions and experience are only properly understood if they are viewed against the background of the time and culture in which they occur.

In later books Erikson elaborates on this theme by detailed psycho-historical studies of Luther[19] and of Gandhi.[20] He is particularly interested in why they came to have the impact which they did. His skill in psychobiography – his capacity to portray configurations of the complex and subtle qualities presented by individual people as well as cultures – seems to draw on his artistic ability as well as on his psychoanalytic skills.

Erikson emphasizes the need to take an integrative approach. In order to understand any action or experience, it is necessary to take into account not only the cultural context in which it occurs but also physio-logical factors and the ego processes which have come to characterize the development of the individual concerned. Each only makes sense in relation to the others. This theme not only provides the rationale for Erikson's seminal book *Childhood and Society* (1950) but is also exempli-fied by his work on *identity*. For him 'the study of identity . . . becomes as strategic in our time as the study of sexuality was in Freud's time'.[21] Erikson explores the processes which underlie our capacity to form a coherent identity. This depends, he argues, on rejections and repudia-tions as well as on identifications. Adolescence is the time when the development of identity becomes of paramount concern. So much of what characterizes this stage of life – intense relationships, cliques, idealism – reflects, he believes, this concern. It is important for young people to have a time free from pressure, a *psychosocial moratorium* as he calls it, to explore possible identities. Otherwise, the risk is increased of identity diffusion, or there may be a premature consolidation leading to an identity crisis in later life.

As is apparent from his focus on integration, Erikson is among those psychoanalysts who have a particular interest in the functioning of the ego – the 'inner synthesis which organises experience and guides action'.[22] His concern, though, is not so much with the defensive measures the ego may adopt but with the processes which make for healthy ego development. In young children he emphasizes the importance of play, 'the infantile form of the human ability . . . to master reality by experiment and planning'.[23] Through play a child can exercise his imagination and experiment with new roles and skills. It enables him to assimilate the patterns and symbols of his society and co-ordinate them with growing skills of bodily and social expression.

Erikson's most notable contribution to ego psychology is his conceptualization of the ego's development throughout life in his notion of the life cycle. He postulates a series of eight stages from birth to death. Each one represents a crisis or turning point, opening up the potential for the development of new ego strengths. Each is characterized by a pair of oppositional tendencies; at the anal stage, for example, these are *autonomy versus shame and doubt*, at adolescence *identity versus role confusion*. From their interplay emerges the pattern of ego qualities which come to characterize that person.

By extending the scope of psychoanalysis, Erikson's writings have attracted the attention of historians and other academics as well as psychologists. His work is also notable for the vivid way he uses case illustrations to reveal how psychoanalytic concepts can illuminate our understanding of both individuals and cultures.[24]

Other Variations

This brief review of the main strands of development of psychoanalytic thought has concentrated only on more notable or divergent forms. There are other more recent developments which, while retaining the basic Freudian approach, have made substantive revisions to portions of the theory. *Heinz Kohut*,[25] for example, has focused on disturbances in the way the self is experienced. He considers (rather like Horney) that these may be expressed in a variety of forms such as an insatiable need for the admiration of others, over-sensitivity to rejection or criticism, or unrealistic idealization of others. Kohut sees the source of such difficulties in the inevitable transition which confronts us in early development, from an infantile state of narcissism, where we experience ourself as the centre of the world to the growing awareness of our separateness and helplessness. Parents can play a key role in supporting the child in this transition by being empathic and responsive. They also help by serving as idealized models with whom the child can identify and feel at one. With their support a child is encouraged to develop mature ambitions and ego ideals which provide a firm grounding for later ability to give meaning to his or her own life. If there is insufficient support, a person may remain rooted in narcissistic vulnerability; and is likely to cope with this either by assuming an infantile grandiosity ('I am the centre of the universe') along with a sense of inferiority, or by an overwhelming need to idealize others in order to find support in their supposed perfection. Kohut is interesting for his clear affirmation that empathy and introspection are the appropriate methods of psychoanalytic investigation. His ideas have created considerable controversy among analysts because of the implications they carry for therapeutic method. The form of the disturbance in the experience of self and the mode of coping with it will become apparent in the nature of the transference relationship with the analyst. But Kohut emphasizes that empathy is not just important in early development but has therapeutic value. Other analysts are concerned that adopting too empathic an attitude may result in undermining the neutrality which they consider essential for the effective analysis of transference.

There has always been some disagreement among psychoanalysts about the precise form which their relationship with a patient should take. For all Freud's insistence on strict neutrality to encourage the transference to the analyst of unconscious and infantile feelings, accounts of even some of his own sessions suggest active therapist involvement.[26] Present-day analysts on the whole probably adopt a more neutral attitude than analysts of Freud's time. They are reluctant to argue, to offer sympathy or blame or any information about themselves for fear of spoiling the transference. There still remains considerable controversy though as to how far this attitude of neutrality should be pursued. There are 'purists'[27] who resist any incursion of strict neutrality. They turn all questions by the patient back on him or herself. If the analyst fails to turn up for the session or even falls asleep during it, that becomes a cause not for apology but for exploring the patient's reactions to the analyst's lapse. While such an attitude may demand considerable self-discipline and be at times stressful for the therapist, the purists believe that it is only in this way that the best therapeutic results can be obtained. As Brenner[28] has pointed out, to express sympathy when a patient has been bereaved may make it that much harder for him to express pleasure or spite at the loss of negative feelings about the person who has died. But other analysts[29] consider that too dispassionate an attitude may disrupt rather than facilitate therapy, for the patient may become too disconcerted or upset by what seems to be the analyst's inhuman indifference. Some[30] advocate a 'therapeutic alliance' whereby part of the interaction is conducted in more normal human terms to provide sufficient reassurance for the patient to accept the necessity of the analyst's neutrality for therapeutic work.

From France has come a controversial development which has been largely ignored by psychoanalysts elsewhere. This is the attempt by *Jacques Lacan* to reinterpret Freudian theory in the light of structuralist linguistics and semiotics (the study of signs). Lacan attracted considerable attention for his flamboyant style and unorthodox approach. His writings[31] are sprinkled with waspish put-downs of other people as well as occasional striking insights. For him psychoanalysis was essentially a tool for understanding rather than for therapy. In spite of his medical background, he was resolutely opposed to it being a medical speciality. He saw it rather as akin to philosophy, anthropology and those disciplines concerned with understanding the human situation. In understanding ourselves with the help of psychoanalysis, we can discover universal laws about humanity and society. Lacan made a stand too against the professionalization of psychoanalysis in France. The point at which an analyst in training becomes ready to practice, he argued, is a question of his own psychological maturity. This can only be assessed by the prospective analyst himself, not by a set of formal criteria. The focus of Lacan's work is on the language of the unconscious and its structures. He was scathing about the development of ego psychology, regarding it as a dilution of the essential achievements of psychoanalysis which he saw as the elaboration of the power of the unconscious and sexuality and its insistence that we are not in rational control of ourselves. Lacan viewed psychoanalytic therapy as an attempt to free the patient by acts of speech. 'Whether it sees itself as an instrument of healing, of formation, or of explanation in depth, psychoanalysis has only a single intermediary: the patient's Word.'[32] Unfortunately for the reader, Lacan's own words are characterized by an inaccessibility which is the opposite of Freud's clarity. He appears to reason that the mysteries of the unconscious justify a seemingly deliberate obscurity in his expression. His extensive use of word-play and puns is not just frivolous, it is claimed, for this mirrors the language of the unconscious. Whether it is necessary to adopt the language of the unconscious for the purpose of analysing its operations would seem to be an arguable matter. It was certainly not an approach favoured by Freud. Even Lacan's most devoted followers admit his 'dense and allusive' style as obstacle. 'His writing is wilfully mysterious and plays upon a syntactic musicality which is not always easy to decode'.[33] Others refer to his 'constitutional ambiguity'[34] and argue that 'to attempt to sum up his thought seems as impertinent an undertaking as to try to translate certain poems'.[35] Whether ideas of lasting value will emerge from his enigmatic work remains to be established.

There are other developments in both personality theory and therapy which while having roots in psychoanalysis have moved firmly outside the fold. *Ronald Laing,* for example, while initially beginning as a psycho-analyst, has been very influenced by existential thought and focuses on the experience of a person and on the complexities arising from relation-ships. We depend on others to validate our sense of self. And yet we cannot ever know what they really think. We can only infer. In our need for others and the failures that can arise from communication with them lie, he believes, many of the seeds of our discontents. More recently, Laing[36] has concerned himself with outranking Rank by speculating on the consequences of intra-uterine life. Could the mother's emotional state, her sense of rejection or acceptance, set up 'resonances' which are communicated to her foetus, thus setting the scene for later orientation to life?

Patterns of Psychoanalytic Thought

The ways in which the main developments diverge from Freud's original ideas can be classified as being of three broad types.

1. Some have counteracted Freud's concern with the first five years of life by emphasizing the significance as well of other phases of the life cycle. So Klein emphasized the first year, Rank the moment of birth and Jung development during the years of maturity.
2. Other theorists, like Adler and the neo-Freudians, have been con-cerned to redress Freud's over-concern with libido and unconscious motivations, and have emphasized the significance of conscious awareness and the functioning of the ego. This development has taken various forms. Some, like Anna Freud and Hartmann have been concerned with extending Freud's original ideas about defence mechanisms and the ego. Others, like Fromm, have moved more to an existential position and have worked from the implica-tions of the human capacity for awareness of existing.
3. The third kind of development is greater concern with the impact of culture on personality. Both Horney and Fromm, for example, have been active in this respect.

Some theorists come into more than one category. Erikson, for example, has developed psychoanalysis in all three of these directions. Not only has he focused on the significance of the ego, but he has traced the changing phases of its development throughout life from childhood to old age and has been concerned to explore its strengths as well as its defences. His theory is also at heart *psychosocial* – he explores the complex ways in which the social context may shape and interact with the sequence of personal development.

Although these variants of Freudian theory differ in their emphases and often also in the concepts which they employ, there are nevertheless basic features which are common to them all. For example, all are dynamic. They accept that behaviour is goal-directed and subject to conflicts which, in turn, influence personality and behaviour. All assume too that behaviour and experience are affected by unconscious motivations and that childhood experience and development have important consequences for adult personality. If the preceding accounts of the different developments of psychoanalytic theory have not been particularly evaluative, it is because they are fundamentally similar in terms of their epistemological status. Much of the general evaluation of the nature of psychoanalytic theory which follows in Part Two will apply to them as well.

It might be thought nevertheless that the existence of differences between them casts doubt on the value of the psychoanalysis in general. How can the specifics of all these different theories be right? But many of the differences are, of course, due to terminology or ways of putting things. Though they may express it very differently, quite often analysts seem to be saying much the same kind of thing. Or differences may be ones of emphasis or elaboration. Freud focused on unconscious motivation and libido theory, because this, for him, was the side of theory about personality which was the least developed. It was not that he was not appreciative of the significance of conscious functioning as well. Some differences are more fundamental. Even these, though, may not necessarily mean that, of two different propositions of this fundamental kind, only one therefore can be correct. For this would presuppose a communality among human beings. And it may reasonably be argued that individuals are even more diverse than theories. Although a theory may have relevance to one individual, it may not have to others. Contradictory theories, therefore, may both be of value. The problem lies more often in the tendency of theorists to over-generalize and to assume that what has proved to be relevant to them and to selected patients is necessarily therefore applicable to all mankind.

Part Two

THE NATURE OF PSYCHOANALYSIS

Having considered what psychoanalysis consists of, we now need to take stock of what kind of animal it is. What sort of theory or contribution to knowledge does it represent? In this appraisal, the focus will be on Freudian theory. For, although psychoanalysis has evolved since Freud's time, his statements of the theory not only remain remarkably influential today, they also contain the essence of the psychoanalytic approach.

CHAPTER 9

Integration and Interpretation

I would suggest that the two most significant features of psychoanalytic theory in terms of contributing to our understanding of social behaviour and experience are the integrative and semantic functions which the theory serves.

Its *integrative* function has already been implied, if not made clear, in the preceding chapter. Psychoanalysis offers a model of the person as a whole. It takes into account the many different sources of our actions and feelings. It provides a way of conceptualizing the various aspects of integration discussed in Chapter 1. So biological and environmental influences and those which come from identifying with other people become id, ego and superego forces. The core of the psychoanalytic view of the human condition is that what we experienced as children remains with us as adults. The tools which psychoanalysis provides are concepts and methods designed to help us penetrate the interplay of multiple determinants and multiple meanings underlying individual integrations. Thus defence mechanisms help us conceive the many ways in which conflicting forces within the person may be integrated. They can be applied to understanding not only conflicts arising from individual frustrations of desire but also our ways of resolving the problems which arise from the nature of human existence. So, for example, an analyst may well be inclined to regard belief in an afterlife in the face of the contradictory evidence of bodily and mental death, as a form of denial – a way of resolving and defending against a conflict, which all humans face in some form, between the will to live and the awareness of eventual death.

This example illustrates also the *semantic* function of psychoanalysis. By this, I mean its role in helping us to interpret the language of the mind; the part it plays in helping us to make sense and become aware of the hidden meaning and rich complexity that underlie the subtleties and paradoxes of actions and mental life. Many other examples have already been given. Dreams, fantasies, mistakes, slips of the tongue, the use of symbolism in language and life all take on new meaning. We listen in a new way to the babble of psychotics, see in a new light the concern of young children with bodily functions, the nature of their play and the content of what they say.

Psychoanalysis teaches us to look beyond the obvious. Choosing to be a dentist may not just be a matter of interests, abilities, coming from the right social background and being in the right place at the right time. We look for its potential psychological significance as well. What a wonderful opportunity, for example, it can provide for the expression of aggression without guilt! This is not to imply that *all* dentists suffer repressed aggression, any more than all dentists are the children of dentists, only that this is one factor which *may* affect choice and contribute to occupational satisfaction.

Psychoanalysis schools us in the logic of irrationality. The paradoxical coexistence of opposites, so common a feature of human actions, begins to become comprehensible. The curious conjunction of cruelty with Christian ideals which characterized the priests of the Inquisition and witch hunters may, at first sight, seem paradoxical. Applying psychoanalytic concepts, it makes 'good sense'. By justifying their actions as being in the pursuit of higher ideals, aggression and even sexual drive could be expressed without conflict with conscience. The frequent attribution of lasciviousness and vicious thoughts and acts to a condemned witch suggests *projection*. This effectively provided the 'justification' for the witch's accusers to torture and pursue her. Even the common method of detecting a witch – pricking pins into every surface of her naked body – suggests more than a hint of *compromise* and symbolic gratification.

In addition to the study of behaviour, psychoanalysis opens up new perspectives on aspects of our culture. The function of myths and fairy stories is one example. Psychoanalysts suggest that the ubiquitous appeal of such stories often lies in the way they symbolize the fundamental conflicts, feelings and desires experienced universally in the normal course of human development. Ancient mythology abounds with parricide, castration, incest and the oral aggression of devouring dragons and monsters. The Oedipal theme is played out not only in the myth from which it took its name but in many others too. Kronos swallowed his own children, castrated his father Uranus and was eventually emasculated in turn by his own son Zeus who had been saved from his father by the help of his mother.

The myths of every people, and not only of the Greeks, are filled with examples of love-affairs between fathers and daughters and even between mothers and sons. Cosmology, no less than the genealogy of royal races, is founded upon incest. For what purpose do you suppose these legends were created? To brand gods and kings as criminals? To fasten on them the abhorrence of the human race? Rather, surely, because incestuous wishes are a primordial human heritage and have never been fully overcome, so that their fulfilment was still granted to gods and their descendants when the majority of common humans were already obliged to renounce them. It is in complete harmony with these lessons of history and mythology that we find incestuous wishes still present and operative in the childhood of the individual.[1]

Fairy stories also, it could be argued, revolve round themes and images which reflect the significance of the young child's world. The frequency with which older figures have opposite characteristics – wicked witch or ugly stepmother as opposed to fairy godmother, evil giant or ogre as opposed to benevolent king – suggests that these may symbolize the ambivalence a child feels towards parental figures. Themes of hostility between young and old are common too – Snow White against her mother, the queen; Hansel and Gretel against the witch; Jack against the giant. Often the young hero's triumph is marked by hacking off the ogre's head. Would it be too fanciful to see in this a gesture of symbolic castration? Themes of mutilation constantly recur. In Grimms' story of Snow White, the evil queen commands her huntsmen to kill her daughter and cut out her lungs and liver so that she might eat them. In Grimms' Cinderella, the ugly stepmother and her daughters, cut off toes and pieces of their feet in order to wear the golden slipper (the prince detects their stratagem by noting the flow of blood staining their stockings).[2] The frequency of such events suggests, at least, that the idea of mutilation is no stranger to children and therefore penis envy and castration anxiety would not be out of place in a child's world. Could even the princess's capacity to sense the pea even though it is tiny and hidden so that no one else can detect it, represent a denial of penis loss and a reassurance that at any rate she can feel the clitoris there even if no one else can see it?

Note too the frequency of oral aggression – the wolf, for example, who threatens to eat little pigs, and, when dressed as her grandmother, Red Riding Hood too. The sometimes sinister consequences of eating is a not uncommon theme – Snow White's poisoned apple, and Hansel and Gretel's gingerbread house are two examples. Could these have called up an unconscious echo in the minds of past generations of children, of infantile conflict when biting the breast caused it to be withdrawn? At least, it may signify the growing child's awareness of the need to control immediate desire. Such interpretations are not meant to imply that the original authors of myths and fairy stories had any *conscious* awareness of their hidden meaning when they devised them; only that, like natural selection, the stories which survived through generations did so because of their capacity to satisfy the unconscious conflicts and emotions of those who heard them.

In his sensitive book *The Uses of Enchantment*,[3] Bruno Bettelheim suggests that fairy tales not only express primary unconscious conflicts but also help children come to terms with them. Their themes signpost directions for growth; for example, needs to transcend dependency, to shift from pleasure to reality principles, to come to terms with separation and to redirect affection from parents to appropriate partners. The Oedipal theme and infantile sexual imagery are common. Jack's beanstalk, springing from Jack's seeds while he sleeps, soars phallic-like into the sky. The fearful threat of the giant he discovers in the castle at the top is an oral one – he will eat Jack if he catches him. But Jack manages to outwit him and steal his magical possessions. He eventually escapes but only with the help of the giant's wife. The giant's death is caused by Jack hacking down the phallic beanstalk. A variety of ways of working through and resolving Oedipal conflicts and achieving mature relationships, Bettelheim argues, are found in different stories. Another common theme is that of integration – the need for co-operation between all aspects of personality. Initiative is important (the ego), but so too is the help of animals (id) and listening to the voice of duty (superego). Because the themes are expressed as symbols and images, the child can register them without necessarily being able to articulate them. And each child can take from the stories the resources he or she needs.

Possibly the kinds of interpretation offered above seem to you far-fetched. If so, I would emphasize again the point made earlier that the experience and world of the infant and the operations of the unconscious are qualitatively different from the conscious world of the average adult. Bodily functions and concrete images from the world about them, not words and abstract thought, dominate the experience of young children and colour the expression of emotion. Their experience is 'egocentric' (in Piaget's sense of the word). It is centred in themselves and their imagination. Fantasy is as significant as reality. To the child, the giant in the storybook is not merely a splodge of colour but, quite possibly, as real and as terrifying as a one-eyed man living next door. I would ask you how else you would explain the themes and images which recur in myth and fairy story and which are so removed from the flavour of reality consciously perceived by an adult?

Conversely, the kinds of interpretation offered by psychoanalysis of behaviour, if not myth and fairy story, may seem obvious to you. Not only are many psychoanalytic-type interpretations anticipated in novels and plays (Shakespeare is a prime example) but they are not that dissimilar to the kinds of inference we may make daily about ourselves and others. This does not, however, invalidate the semantic contribution of psychoanalysis. It would be surprising if people in their daily life and writers, especially those of genius, had not discovered something of the language of the mind. The particular value of psychoanalysis is the depth to which it has probed and the systematic formulation it has provided of this language. Remember also that Freudian ideas, if only in superficial form, have become absorbed into our culture. In this way, they have become part of the armoury of concepts with which we interpret and construe our world.

I have argued then that, in addition to the comprehensive, integrative conception of the person it provides, the main value of the psycho-analysis is semantic – the provision of meaning. Psychoanalysis is clearly capable of providing *an* interpretation. It certainly has the potential to elicit meaning in the form of complex and differentiated accounts of actions, experience and the products of human minds. The key question is, though, how can we be sure that the interpretations it provides are accurate? This question takes on particular significance in view of the varieties and complexities of meaning which, according to psycho-analytic theory, may underlie even the most seemingly straight-forward action. It may mean what it seems to mean, precisely the opposite or something different altogether. An action may mean two or three things at the same time. How can we tell what meaning it really has? How do we know, for example, whether a hostile action is the straightforward expression of aggression, aggression displaced from some other target, or even a reaction formation, signifying underlying feelings of liking or desires which, for some reason, cause conflict if directly expressed?

There is unfortunately no easy test. Close scrutiny of the behaviour in question may help. If the aggression is a reaction formation, for example, then it is quite likely to be slightly overdone and to have an artificial ring about it. There may be aspects or nuances of behaviour inconsistent with the aggressive pose. Underlying feelings may show through in small gestures, the use of words or when the person is offguard – when tired, for example, or after a few drinks. As we have seen, the analyst can employ dream interpretation and free association to yield further clues. The analyst's task is then to feel for a consistent pattern. It is generally difficult and usually impossible to interpret a single action on its own. Any interpretation is but a working hypothesis to be judged in terms of its consistency with the total pattern of actions and experience.

This procedure is by no means unique to psychoanalysis. In everyday life we are continually making sense of a situation by feeling for its pattern. The advantage of psychoanalysis is that it extends our capacity to do this. Both obscure as well as ordinary manifestations of feeling and action can be made intelligible. The fact that John seems to snap his sister's head off for no apparent reason can be made sense of if we know that he has just quarrelled with his girl-friend and if we are familiar with the concept of displacement. Antonia's apparently odd oscillations between chaotic untidiness and obsessive order can be seen as consistent enough when we think of this as a residue of anal conflict between a delight in messiness and the imposed need to do things at the proper time and place.

One of the difficulties of feeling for the pattern in this way, particularly if we employ psychoanalytic concepts, is that many of the parts and links in the pattern are inevitably hypotheses or open to more than one interpretation. To take up the jigsaw analogy used earlier, a lot of the pieces have alternative or flexible shapes. This not only renders the task of fitting them together very problematic but makes it difficult to be sure that the pattern we eventually arrive at is the appropriate one.

Interpretation is a skill, an art, not a mechanical procedure of matching a single meaning to a single manifestation. The complexity and difficulty of interpretation and the fact that there is no straightforward test of its validity, leaves it open to abuse. However, the existence of dubious interpretations and the tendency sometimes encountered to treat interpretation as definitive do not, in themselves, invalidate psychoanalysis any more than the fundamental tenets of Christianity are impugned by the behaviour of poor Christians. They do, however, arouse concern about the scientific status of psychoanalytic theory.

CHAPTER 10

Psychoanalysis as Science

Psychoanalytic interpretation depends on the application of a set of concepts and procedures (like free association and dream work) for deriving latent from manifest meanings. These in turn depend, in part at least, on a set of propositions which purport to explain why certain characteristics or behaviours come about. So, for example, the concept of anal character rests on a proposition about the influence of a particular type of infantile experience on adult personality. Freud often states or implies that such methods, concepts and propositions were derived primarily from his observations of patients in therapy. How far is this true? And what kind of basis could observations of this kind provide for his theory?

Erich Fromm, himself an experienced analyst, has argued that the process of psychoanalysis is 'exquisitely scientific'. He points out that it involves making detailed observations, deriving inferences and formulating hypotheses on the basis of these, and then proceeding to test these hypotheses or, at least, to check how plausible they are.

> I have listened to a patient for thirty hours. I have heard some of his dreams. I form a hypothesis. His next thirty hours, his next thirty dreams, will prove or disprove my assumptions. I form a new hypothesis. I get more material, and eventually whatever further information comes forth from him will or will not make sense in terms of my hypothesis . . . I can analyse a person for a while and know that I do not understand him. Then, after perhaps six months more of analysis, a point arrives when everything clicks – I see it. 'Yes, this is really the structure; this makes me understand why he developed the symptoms.'[1]

One of the difficulties of evaluating such claims is that detailed transcripts of psychoanalytic sessions are not readily available. The philosopher B. F. Farrell though has recently made a very interesting analysis[2] based on transcripts of sessions between P. M. Turquet of the Tavistock Institute and a seventeen-year-old boy referred because of academic underachievement. It is true that therapists differ in their approach and there is no reason to suppose that Turquet worked in the same way as Fromm or Freud. But Farrell does point to a number of features which seem likely to be common to all analytic sessions. He paints a very different picture from Erich Fromm.

He regards the patient's situation in therapy as an ambiguous one which is likely to arouse his anxiety. The patient is given no direct guidance on how to react. He does not know what is expected of him and any queries or challenges he makes are turned back on him by further questions. The therapist–patient relationship is deliberately designed to encourage transference and suggestibility. It is very probable that what the patient says will be partly shaped by the reinforcement provided by the reactions and expressions of interest of the analyst. If only directly, the patient will be encouraged to choose themes on the basis of their capacity to elicit a response from his analyst and to talk and think about these in a way which is consistent with the interpretations introduced. In effect, Farrell is suggesting that the analytic method is not so much a method of discovery but is, to some extent at least, a self-confirmatory way of creating the facts it purports to find.

The views of both Fromm and Farrell, although different in their conclusions, seem to imply that facts are (or can be) there for the finding – that they *can* be derived or confirmed by 'objective' observation. But, as was pointed out in Chapter 1, no theory or observation is a mere reflection of reality. All discovery and understanding involves construction. Any investigation requires us to choose what we look at and how, it requires that we select a perspective and categories for conceptualizing and describing it. Just as a physicist constructs special instruments for measuring what interest him so a psychoanalyst might argue he needs to get his patient to talk about certain things in a particular way in order to bring to light the information he seeks.

Nevertheless, it may still seem that there is something peculiarly tautological about psychoanalysis if, on one hand, the concepts are supposed to be derived from observations of patients and, on the other, they are necessary before such observations can be made. In response to this criticism, we will need first to question to what extent Freud's ideas really *have* been derived in this way. Secondly, we need to bear in mind that, as the work of Piaget has made clear, this process of lifting yourself up by your own bootstraps is characteristic of the development of our understanding in general. In Piaget's terms, it involves both *assimilation* – ordering what is perceived in terms of your existing constructs; and *accommodation* – where necessary modifying those concepts to best deal with the world as experienced. A useful analogy for these mutual processes is a filing system. Incoming items are sorted to fit the existing categories (assimilation) but, as the system evolves, so it will be revised and new categories will be created to make finer or more effective differentiations (accommodation). We can think of the development of Freud's theory in this way. He began by trying to make sense of what his patients told him in terms of concepts, distinctions and ways of thinking available to an educated physiologist of the time. These would have been culled not just from science and medicine but from everyday life and his knowledge of languages, philosophy, other cultures and the arts. Most of the central assumptions of psychoanalysis did not originate with Freud. As we have already seen, the power of the unconscious had been first demonstrated clinically to Freud by Charcot and Bernheim and later by Breuer. The significance of unconscious thought had been anticipated by several writers before Freud, especially Schopenhauer and Nietzsche. Lancelot Whyte in *The Unconscious Before Freud*[3] concludes that 'the general conception of unconscious mental processes was . . . *topical* around 1800, and *fashionable* around 1870–80 . . . It cannot be disputed that by 1870–1880 the general conception of the unconscious mind was a European commonplace, and that many special applications of this general idea had been vigorously discussed for several decades'.[4] Whyte points out that Nietzsche had invented the word 'id' and made mention of sublimation. As noted earlier, Freud's ideas of instinct had been influenced by Darwin's theory of evolution. When Freud was only sixteen, Maudsley[5] had suggested that sexuality is the root of social feelings, and Krafft-Ebing[6] had later proclaimed it as the source of altruism and of moral and expression. Freud's bitter rival Moll[7] wrote about the stages of sexual development of children eight years before the publication of the *Three Essays on Sexuality*. Five years before, Havelock Ellis[8] had described the pleasure which children experience from oral and anal stimulation and had drawn a vivid analogy between breast feeding and adult sexual union.[9] The Oedipal theme, of course, is to be found in myth and literature, and Shakespeare's works (as well as those of other writers) also resonate with examples of defensive processes like projection, reaction formation and undoing.

All this is not in any way to decry Freud's achievement. It was not that he plagiarized his predecessors but rather that, like almost all scientific advances, his contribution was to use, and in so doing transform, what was already extant. The ingredients were there. But it was Freud's especial genius to extend, elaborate and link the elements into a coherent theory. And where this was inadequate to assimilate his observations then he modified it. Psychoanalytic theory was not static. Through progressive assimilations and accommodations Freud's theory evolved throughout his lifetime. So he discarded his early seduction theory. He revised his theory of instincts to include aggression. His emphasis on the significance of libido theory shifted to take ego processes more into account.

The essential point then I am stressing here is that Freud's theories are not to be regarded, as Freud sometimes seems to suggest, as derived purely from his observations of his patients and himself. But neither are they to be seen as entirely self-confirmatory constructions imposed on his data regardless of their nature. His ideas represent complex integrations based on a wide range of knowledge and ideas and applied by him to make sense of what his patient told him. It was their effectiveness in this task that, to some extent at least, then provided the grounds for their development and modification.

One of the greatest strengths of the procedures of orthodox science is their ability to make *explicit* effectiveness of this kind – in other words, to demonstrate unambiguously the fit between a theory and what it purports to explain. It is in this respect that the scientific status of psychoanalysis is open to question. For a start, we have no record of Freud's original data. We are not able to judge for ourselves how well his interpretations work. We are forced to take on trust his judgement or reject it. Farrell's analysis of Turquet's sessions shows how transcripts can help us to gauge the nature of what goes on. Even with their help, though, it is arguable as to how far we would be in a position to assess the fit. For the data which concern Freud were not constituted by the words themselves but by their meanings, that is to say by the interpretations placed on them. These are not unambiguously present in a transcript but have to be wrested from it. The meanings which should be attributed to particular acts or utterances are often likely to be open to dispute. The problems of applying the normal criteria of scientific procedure when meanings are the subject matter are discussed in the next chapter.

We have further reasons to be cautious of Freud's assertion about the support his observations provide for his ideas. He took no notes during analytic sessions. Rightly perhaps, he regarded this as likely to interfere with the therapeutic relationship between himself and his patient. But this means that he had to rely on recollection and on notes made after the session had ended, making it more possible that he might select what was congruent with his thesis and ignore that which was not. Nor does Freud provide us with other information relevant to his theory. Much of his explanation of adult behaviour is premised on suppositions about what happens during the early years of life. He claims to have based these initially on the recollections of his patients of their childhood experiences of some 20 to 30 years before. The dangers of reconstructing infantile experience in this way is exemplified by Freud's seduction theory. At first, he assumed that most of his patients had been seduced as children. Only later did he realize that the majority of such memories were fantasy. In *The Question of Lay-Analysis*[10] he does claim confidently that, 'afterwards, we undertook analysis on children themselves, and it was no small triumph when we were thus able to confirm in them everything that we had been able to divine, in spite of the amount to which it had been overlaid and distorted in the interval'.[11] But the only account of the analysis of a child in Freud's own work is the case of Little Hans.[12] And, as was indicated in Chapter 2, this was not carried out by Freud himself but by the boy's father with Freud's guidance. Nowhere does Freud provide detailed, direct observations of children of the kind that might convince us of the developmental pattern he asserts.

Freud's logic too is sometimes open to question. In the previous chapter, it was pointed out that his concept of *Thanatos* rested on a chain of somewhat shaky arguments. Wittgenstein[13] has also criticized Freud's reasoning that dreams nearly always represent the expression of a wish, albeit in disguised form. He points out that if you are preoccupied by something like a sexual problem then, no matter where you start, even if it be with the objects that just happen to be on the table or with someone else's dream, free association is likely to take you back eventually to your preoccupation. Thus a train of free association leading from a dream to an unconscious desire may tell you something about the person concerned but it does not demonstrate, as Freud assumed, that that desire was why the dream occurred.

Such doubts as these do indicate the need for more explicit demonstration of the validity of psychoanalytic ideas. Unfortunately, most psychoanalysts have followed Freud's lead. They have regarded the theory as being adequately 'proved upon the couch' and have been inclined to question the appropriateness of a more formal kind of test. Given the induction and training which every analyst has to undergo, this is perhaps hardly surprising. He or she will probably have been carefully selected from several applicants. He will then spend a number of years in personal analysis. Through this long and quite probably sometimes painful process he will arrive at a new understanding of himself. The insights and ways of thinking acquired along the way are put into practice daily. They provide the frame for his work with his own patients and, quite possibly, for his awareness of his personal relationships too. On one hand, you might, as psychoanalysts do, consider that all this places him in a privileged position. He is better able to judge the power of the theory because he has seen it working in practice. On the other hand, you may consider, as Farrell does, that it renders him 'personally and professionally committed to the presupposition that psychoanalysis is an authentic experience',[14] and that it would be too much to expect him to contemplate that it could be otherwise.[15]

Psychologists have stepped in where psychoanalysts have not deigned to tread. Many attempts have been made to test propositions which relate to psychoanalytic theory by experiment and by other kinds of investigations such as observation and cross-cultural comparison. Very useful summaries and reviews of such studies and the problems they pose have been provided by Fisher and Greenberg[16] and by Paul Kline.[17] The scientific testing of hypotheses depends on providing or creating observable situations which will either confirm or refute the idea in question. The concern of psychoanalysis with meaning as a subject matter often makes this difficult to do. The problem is compounded by the nature of psychoanalytic concepts and propositions, a feature which will be expanded upon shortly. Nevertheless, the number of relevant studies runs into thousands. As one might expect of such a complex theory which yields an array of potential hypotheses, some fare better than others and some have not been adequately tested at all. While it would be inappropriate to attempt to review such studies in any detail here, the pages which follow provide an overview of the kind of support they yield. In particular, I will try to throw into relief the problems confronting investigations of this kind. Freud's ideas are discussed in the order in which they were presented in Part One.

Not surprisingly, it is not easy to obtain solid support for Freud's theory of the *unconscious*. Its very nature indicates its elusiveness. Its workings remain hidden from conscious view and are manifest only in distorted and indirect form. The most relevant research is work on dreams. For Freud, as we have seen, dreams were the royal road to the unconscious. In particular, they are expressions of unrealized wishes. Very occasionally, these are directly represented. More often they are disguised by the distortions of dream work (i.e., condensation, displacement, etc). In this way, a repressed desire can be given partial expression while avoiding anxiety which might disrupt sleep. Another function of dreams then is to preserve sleep. One problem in testing this theory is that it is not always clear precisely what Freud intended. For example, he claimed that while events of the previous day often crop up in the content of dreams, their real significance is the vehicle they provide for the disguised representation of conflicts and desires rooted in childhood experience. But, as Jones[18] has pointed out, almost all the examples which Freud provides in *The Interpretation of Dreams,* have their meaning rooted in disturbing wishes in the *present* life experience of the adult dreamer.

Two primary kinds of evidence have been brought to bear on this theory. The first consist of investigations of the reported content of dreams – Hall and his co-workers, for example, have collected and compared several thousand dreams and other studies have explored the effects of different manipulations or contextual situations on the content reported. The second source of evidence comes from the laboratory research on dreaming which has flourished since the late 1950s, where subjective reports are supplemented by physiological recordings and observations of sleepers.

What is very evident from the content analysis studies (and as practically any dreamer will confirm) is that the reported or manifest content of dreams is nearly always psychologically meaningful. People, places and objects make their appearance, many of them identifiable by the dreamer. Actions take place, often in specific locations and the dream may be coloured by emotional feeling. Several investigators have developed systems to categorize the kinds of theme and content that occur. It is also quite apparent that what happens to a person prior to sleep can affect what goes on in his dreams. An erotic film, for example, has been found to increase the amount of symbolic sexual content;[19] while one involving body mutilation was more likely to produce anxiety themes.[20] Even undergoing stressful group psychotherapy can increase the incidence of disturbing dreams.[21] What happens while a person is sleeping can also influence what they dream about – sometimes in quite subtle ways. If a sleeper is played a tape recording of his own voice, for example, it seems that the figures in his dreams will be more likely to be recalled as being active and assertive than if the recording is of the same words spoken by someone else.[22] The experiences of pregnancy and menstruation as well as taking certain drugs are other factors known to be capable of affecting what is dreamed. Differences in typical dream content have also been reported from subjects of different ages,[23] race and class[24] and between men and women.[25] While these are usually explicable in terms of cultural roles and different life experiences, attempts have been made to relate sex differences to Freud's theory of psychosexual development. Thus, Hall and Van de Castle[26] interpret their observation that men are more likely to dream of physical injury or defect as possible evidence of their greater concern with castration anxiety consistent with Freud's idea of the Oedipus complex.

While dream content is clearly often meaningful and related to life experiences, there is no evidence that it largely represents unrealized desires. Rather, it seems to be a forum for expression of many kinds of preoccupation and concern. Nor is there much evidence from dream research of defensive distortion or that dreams work to preserve sleep. Patients waiting to undergo surgery report, if anything, increased levels of anxiety in their dreams,[27] and as Fisher and Greenberg[28] point out, if you gently disturb an individual who is in dreamless sleep, this does not prompt him to begin to dream. Along with Hall and Van de Castle,[29] they are inclined to reject the usefulness of Freud's distinction between manifest and latent content. Among other support for their view, they cite a finding by Reis[30] that much the same kind of meaning is elicited from the straightforward analysis of the manifest content of a dream on its own as when free association to get at latent content is used as well. Support though for the idea that meanings *can* be carried in symbolic form has come from several studies. Investigations of Freud's idea of sexual symbolism have found that subjects do tend to ascribe appropriate genders to objects which Freud considered likely to serve as sexual symbols (e.g., sticks, rolling pins, caves etc.). Indirect support also comes from the fact that languages which attribute gender to nouns also broadly tend to conform to this pattern[31] though the relationship is not at all precise, a fact which Kline and others see as due to the many factors which underlie the assignment of gender in language.

One early result of the laboratory studies of dreams which turned out to be the cornerstone of much subsequent research, was the discovery of REM sleep. During the course of a night's sleep, several periods occur when the sleeper engages in rapid eye movements (REM) behind closed eyelids. Subjects woken up during these period are more likely to report that they are in the middle of a dream that when there is no REM activity. (Interestingly, penile erection has also been found to accompany REM periods.[32] This may have a physiological basis due to associated activity in the limbic area of the brain. But, as the strength of the erections seems to be related to the erotic content of the accompanying dreams[33] you may regard this as compatible, at least, with a wish-fulfilling and sexual function of dreams.) The REM studies most relevant to Freud's theory are those which have induced REM deprivation. Each time REM patterns are observed, the sleeper is woken. Depriving a sleeper of REM sleep in this way generally leads (though there are some individual variations) to increased REM activity when the subject is eventually allowed to sleep undisturbed.[34] It seems likely that this increase reflects a greater need to dream, for deprivation subjects who report that they are in the middle of a dream when their REM sleep is disrupted seem to show less need later for compensatory REM sleep.[35] There is some evidence also, though other studies have not always confirmed this, that extensive REM deprivation leads to disturbances in perception[36] and a greater tendency for unconscious wishes to break through in response to projective tests.[37] All this seems consistent with the notion that we *need* to dream and that this may be because one important function of dreams is to allow us to express unconscious tensions.

In conclusion, the general pattern of findings in this area is broadly consistent with Freud's notion that dreams provide an important reflection and necessary expression of mental life. But the kinds of meaning found in dreams and the way they are expressed appear to be much more variable than the specific proposals of his theory would suggest.

When we come to Freud's theory of *psychosexual development*, the first thing we might do is what Freud failed to – consider whether there is any evidence from direct observations of children which confirm a developmental pattern of the kind he postulated. The classic studies of Arnold Gesell[38] of the natural behaviour of children of different ages do indicate that they go through a sequence in which the focus of their interest shifts from mouth to anus to genitals. The pleasure which young babies get from sucking does also seem to be independent of its role in nutrition.[39] While evidence is lacking that the anus also becomes a source of pleasure, this is probably only because social conventions have inhibited research. It is certainly an area which is highly sensitive to stimulation.[40] Although he accepts that there is a sequence of shifting interests of the kind that Freud suggests, Farrell[41] has taken exception to viewing the pleasures obtained from such stimulation as sexual and consequently labelling the areas concerned as erotogenic. But kissing is commonly an important mode of adult sexual interaction and anal stimulation, while more inhibited due to its conventional associations with shame and disgust, may well be involved too. In male homosexuality it often plays a central role. Given the significance of all three areas in the adult sexual act and a relation, as Freud supposed, between the course of childhood gratification and the form that adult sexual satisfactions take, there seems every reason to distinguish by the label 'erotic' these pleasures from other kinds which a child may receive. Indeed it might well be considered that linking them together in a coherent conceptualization in this way was Freud's especial contribution.

What of the effects of psychosexual development? You will remember from Chapter 4 that Freud believed that fixation at infantile stages of development not only affected adult sexuality but was also an important source of neurosis and personality characteristics. A feature of his theory is that it makes predictions which are difficult to account for on any other basis. The 'anal' character, for example, is seen as a very particular combination of traits. He is orderly, stubborn and parsimonious, often obsessive and sometimes a shade sadistic or concerned with creative work. Research has been directed at checking whether the combinations the theory predicts do commonly exist. A typical strategy would be to administer questionnaires to large numbers of subjects and to see if the correlations predicted between traits obtain. One problem with this approach is that the theory does not imply that all the traits necessarily come together in any one person. It allows too for the possibility of oscillation between opposite traits (e.g. tidiness–disorder) as a result of defensive reactions. There is also a problem of devising questionnaires which can be considered to be reliable measures of the characteristics concerned.[42] Another approach is through experiment. Lerner,[43] working on the assumption that collecting represents a sublimation of the wish to hold on to faeces, found that adolescent stamp collectors were more sensitive to anal stimuli than other boys of the same age. And in a study of Rosenwald[44] subjects adjudged as anal were more reluctant to make large bets (i.e. were more parsimonious) in a gambling game. After reviewing a variety of evidence of both types, Kline,[45] and Fisher and Greenberg[46] conclude that there is good support for the existence of an anal syndrome.

Freud himself was far less clear about the consequences for personality of fixation at the oral stage. His colleague Abraham[47] did enlarge on this apparently with Freud's approval. He distinguished between the effects of the oral passive stage where sucking is the predominant mode and the active stage where this is supplanted by biting. The oral characteristics he suggested include concern with dependency and nurturance (being looked after), liking to be with others, tendency to extremes of optimism or pessimism, openness to new ideas and experiences, restlessness and impatience and concern with oral gratification (smoking, sucking or chewing sweets, drinking, talking etc). Some support for the existence of a syndrome of this sort is provided by the research literature. As but three examples – questionnaire studies do show some clustering of characteristics according to prediction; oral behaviour has been cor-related with dependency in nursery children;[48] and oral types seem to condition more easily when rewarded with sweets or social approval, whereas anals respond best to money.[49] But, as both Kline and Fisher and Greenberg agree, the evidence in support is by no means as clear-cut as that for the anal character.

The critical question is how far can such characteristics be related, as psychoanalysts suppose, to the experiences of childhood. Research on this issue is problematic for several reasons. The theory postulates that overindulgence *and* deprivation can both induce fixation. Freud also supposed that constitutional factors may play a part in predisposing sensitivity at a particular developmental stage. This makes it very difficult to set up an unambiguous test of the effects of rearing. There is difficulty too in obtaining adequate accounts of childhood. Most retrospective studies have had to rely on parents' recollections of how they brought up their children – data which are quite likely to be unre-liable.[50] In any case, one might suppose that it was the *experience* of the infant which was significant rather than the particular rearing practices employed. Another problem arises from the variety of methods which are used to establish the presence of oral or anal tendencies. They include not only questionnaires about habits, interests and food preferences, but also observations of behaviour (e.g., biting nails, chewing pencils etc). A popular method is the projective test. The number of oral images a subject gives in response to an inkblot may be noted, for example. In the frequently used Blacky test, subjects are asked to make up stories about pictures of a puppy portrayed in a variety of situations including suckling and one where he is blindfold with a knife poised over his tail. Stories are scored for oral, anal and Oedipal (e.g. castration anxiety) concerns. The difficulty is being sure of how adequate a measure such observations and tests are and how far they can be considered to be comparable. Yet another problem is created by the fact that personality attributes are influenced by many factors. Social conventions, for example, may make it less easy for males to display or admit dependency behaviour. Such influences may obscure the effects of psychosexual development and may account for the results of several studies which have found an effect predicted by psychoanalytic theory with subjects of one sex but not of the other.

Not surprisingly, in spite of the considerable research effort expended, overall results have been disappointing. Few studies, either retrospective or longitudinal, have been able to demonstrate a clear-cut relationship between feeding or toilet training practices and later personality. There is what might be regarded as a little indirect support from cross-cultural research. Whiting and Child[51] analysed ethnographic data from over seventy societies. They found evidence that people from societies which show concern over oral socialization are also more likely to attribute illness to oral sources (e.g., to contamination from kissing or eating). A similar relationship centred on negative anal fixation was not significant. Support then for a specific relationship between oral and anal fixations and later characteristics is sparse. However, as Kline[52] is at pains to point out, given the formidable difficulties of finding adequate measures and designing effective studies in this area, the lack of confirming evidence, or even the failure of a study to support a specific hypothesis, does not in itself necessarily constitute refutation of Freud's ideas.

As observed in Chapter 4, it is the Oedipal stage which, Freud believed, carries most significance for the child and later the adult that child will become. His writings about the nature of the Oedipus complex form a collection of hypotheses rather than a single idea. He postulates that childrens' feelings for their parents begin to change at about the age of four or five. From the initial primary affection for their mother, both boys and girls come to develop greater interest in the parent of the opposite sex and hostility for the one who is the same. A particular problem for a boy is the emotional turmoil, including a fear of castration, created by his sense of rivalry with his father for the affection of his mother. The way this conflict is resolved produces lasting changes in personality and sexual and emotional attitudes, and at this stage the seeds of neurosis may be sown.

Freud and Psychoanalysis

Testing such hypotheses is not only open to all the methodological problems which have been noted in the preceding paragraphs but yet others as well. Several studies have found, for example, that direct questioning of children reveals no particular preference for either parent. Friedman[53] has argued that the failure to find a difference may be because of defensive measures used to protect the ego against the intense anxiety created by Oedipal concerns. The emotions and conflicts created by this phase of development will only be operative at an unconscious level. When, instead of asking direct questions, Friedman analysed the stories which children made up in response to pictures of a father and child, he did find significantly more hostility expressed against the man in the responses of the boys. He also found that girls were much more likely to include father going up the stairs and entering a room. In psychoanalytic terms, as he points out, both images symbolize sexual intercourse.

Considerable subtlety has been exercised in designing studies to tap such elusive subject matter. As we have seen, Hall has approached it through the systematic analysis of dream content. In a series of studies[54] comparing the dreams of men and women students, he found that men were more likely to dream of male strangers and that these were more likely to be aggressive encounters. There were also significantly more instances in male dreams of content symbolic of castration and anxiety.[55] Friedman too has claimed results consistent with Freud's idea of castration anxiety. As part of the studies referred to above,[56] he gave boys and girls between the ages of five and sixteen, unfinished stories to complete. Each had a theme with the potential to arouse castration associations (e.g. a child comes in to find his elephant broken, a monkey is in danger of losing its tail). In the boys' completions, he found *fewer* castration-type references at ages five and thirteen when anxiety might be expected to be at its peak. There was no difference in the number of responses made by girls at these compared with other ages. He took this as indicative of a defensive reaction by the boys against the intense anxiety created by castration fears.

The ingenuity of work in this area is further demonstrated by a study by Sarnoff and Corwin.[57] They worked on the assumption that fear of death could be regarded as a generalization of castration anxiety. Interestingly, they found that in male subjects with high castration anxiety (as assessed by the Blacky test) sexual arousal produced a significant increase in responses indicative of fear of death. This they considered to be consistent with the Oedipus idea. Other investigators have adopted a cross-cultural approach. Boys from an Israeli kibbutz, for example, who tend to receive less contact with their parents than is usual in a family, were adjudged to have significantly less castration anxiety[58] and, in a detailed re-analysis of the ethnographic material used by

Whiting and Child, Stephens[59] found a close relationship between the presence in a society of cultural conventions which are likely to intensify the Oedipal situation for boys, and indices of sexual anxiety among the adult males.

Findings like those above cannot be taken as totally unambiguous support for the Oedipus theory. Farrell[60] has suggested that socialization into the standard sex roles of Western society might in itself be likely to lead to boys experiencing greater hostility than girls in their relationship with father. Given too the greater likelihood of boys engaging in rough and tumble play, it would not be surprising if they should exhibit at an unconscious level more concern with body injury. In line with this argument, dream content involving inability to do something, which Hall has interpreted as indicative of castration anxiety, might be better seen as expressive of the greater pressure on males in our society to take an active role. Nevertheless, the range of evidence about childrens' feelings towards their parents and for castration anxiety is impressive and does seem to fit the predictions of Freudian theory.

There are other hypotheses associated with the Oedipus idea. Freud suggested that at this stage the developmental paths of boys and girls diverge. He ascribes the origins of superego development in boys to the increased identification with their fathers which he sees as the way most boys come to master Oedipal conflict. Girls are more preoccupied by the awareness that they lack a penis, and the emergence of their superego depends more on their fear of loss of love. There is little support for such hypotheses. Freud assumed that a boy's identification comes about largely through fear. But most studies (at least from our culture) suggest that it is a caring, nurturant attitude on the part of the father that fosters the strongest identification and the development of firm moral principles. Fisher and Greenberg, at least, take such findings to imply that:

> a formal revision seems in order that would conceptualize the resolution of the Oedipal crisis in the male as occurring not primarily out of anxiety but rather on the basis of trust . . . The boy . . . gives up his acute competitive stance *vis-à-vis* father because father transmits friendly positive messages inviting him to join up rather than fight.[61]

Although there is evidence which does suggest that women are more sensitive to rejection than men, this may as well be due to differential sex role socialization in our culture as to the Oedipal dynamics which Freud suggests. One study has found that after an examination fewer women students than men returned the pencils they had borrowed.[62] The investigator claimed, perhaps rather tongue-in-cheek, that this result *could* be considered consistent with penis envy. But more serious studies have as yet found little evidence of substance for this concept.

Finally, in relation to Freud's theory of psychosexual development, it is worth noting that there is a good deal of support, both from animal and human studies, for his general notion of the critical significance of early experience. Harlow[63] has found that depriving rhesus monkeys of normal relationships in infancy produces profound and lasting disturbances of later social, sexual and maternal behaviours. Bowlby[64] in an extensive review of studies of children whose parental relationships had been severely disrupted during the first five years of life, also concludes that experiences during this time have lasting significance. Although some of Bowlby's initial interpretations have come under fire,[65] his general conclusion about the importance of early attachments would still appear to hold.

Evaluation of studies bearing on Freud's theory of psychosexual development is fraught with difficulty. Support for several specific hypotheses is lacking and others are clearly in need of revision. The evidence, however, is at least broadly consistent with Freud's general contention that the emotional development of children is closely bound up with the changing patterns of their body needs, and that there is a correlation between early experience and later personality. The precise nature of that relationship remains to be confirmed.

Formal empirical support for Freud's later ideas on *psychodynamics* – the third area of psychoanalytic theory covered in Part One – can be dealt with more briefly. What work there is has been largely on mechanisms of defence. Most of this has been directed at the effect of repression on cognitive and perceptual processes. Wilkinson and Carghill[66] showed, for example, that stories with an Oedipal theme were more difficult to recall than more neutral ones even though both kinds of story had been largely equated for difficulty. And Levinger and Clark[67] found that associations given to words which had emotional connotations were more difficult for subjects to remember than those which had been given to neutral words. Both studies have been taken as experimental demonstrations of repression. Several studies have claimed to show perceptual defence – that is, that emotionally-arousing stimuli are more difficult to detect. The problem with some of the first experiments of this kind was that their results could be explained without the need to invoke repression. The effect found may have been due, for example, to the greater unfamiliarity of the emotional words, or subjects may have been more inhibited in repeating them aloud because of their taboo nature. Fortunately, several experiments[68] have ingeniously circumvented such confounding factors and have clearly demonstrated that perceptual defence does exist. Blum,[69] in particular, in a series of careful studies using the Blacky pictures, has shown that it comes into operation much as psychoanalytic theory might predict – i.e., when subjects who are inclined to use repression as a defence are confronted with stimuli which arouse conflict.

The only other mechanism of defence to receive much attention from experimenters has been *displacement*. One approach to this has been stimulated by Dollard and his colleagues' elaboration of the idea that when people are frustrated they become aggressive.[70] Experiments have shown that when the aggression cannot be directed at the source of the frustration, it may be displaced elsewhere. For example, boys at a summer camp who had been forced to miss a film because a boring testing session had run overtime, were found to express much more negative attitudes towards Mexican and Japanese people than they had before.[71]

Freud's explanations of the different forms of *neurosis* and *mental disorder* have collected less empirical support than any of the areas reviewed so far. They have proved the most difficult nut for the experimentalist to crack. To some extent, this is due to ambiguity in the original ideas. Suggestions about the aetiology of mental disturbance are scattered through his works and precise hypotheses are not always easy to assemble. It is partly also because the ideas are particularly difficult to test. For example, one clear-cut suggestion he made is that paranoia is closely linked to repressed homosexuality. This idea emerged from Freud's detailed analysis[72] of a book by a lawyer, Daniel Schreber which described his personal experience of becoming a paranoid schizophrenic (a state which involves delusions of persecution). Freud reasoned that the origins of his condition lay in a childhood Oedipal conflict in which, due to fear of castration, he had become fixated on the notion of sexual submission to his father. A series of defensive manoeuvres protected the adult Schreber from awareness of this unconscious desire. These involved converting it into its opposite – hatred – then projecting and displacing this, which resulted in him seeing other people as hating him. If such a scenario strikes you as rather complicated and a little odd, it is not my intention here to enlarge on it or defend Freud's reasoning. The purpose is rather to point to the difficulty of testing such an idea. To do this presumably must involve finding a measure not just of homosexuality but of *repressed* homosexuality. In fact, a study by Zamansky[73] claimed to have achieved just this and to have confirmed the link with paranoia. In an experiment presented as a visual estimation task, he found that male patients classified as paranoid, when compared with other schizophrenic patients, spent more time looking at pictures of males than of females. (He had already demonstrated such a preference effect to be characteristic of homosexuals.) But, when subjects were asked to indicate which picture they preferred or when the male pictures had clear homosexual connotations, both situations in which their defences would be called into play, there was no difference between the two groups. Zamansky had in fact hypothesized that here the paranoids would show less attraction but the results are still in line with the basic idea. In other words, the results suggest paranoid schizophrenics follow a homosexual preference pattern but only in situations where defences are likely to be relaxed.

Freud claims to have derived most of his ideas from his work with patients. And there is no doubt that psychoanalysis has profoundly influenced the practice and thought of psychiatrists including those who remain unconvinced of its value. Even allowing for the logical and methodological difficulties involved, it does seem rather paradoxical therefore to find such a dearth of adequate investigations in this area. As the reviews of Kline and of Fisher and Greenberg confirm, support is the exception rather than the rule. There is far more evidence consistent with the psychoanalytic account of normal personality functioning than with its specific explanations of mental disorder.

Before leaving this consideration of evidence consistent with psychoanalytic theory, mention should be made of two approaches of a rather different kind. One is the attempt to devise computer models of psychoanalytic conceptions of psychological processes. Colby,[74] for example, who is a practising analyst as well as being well versed in computer modelling techniques, has devised a programme to simulate 'neurotic process'. Essentially, this represents a set of beliefs, each with a particular emotional charge. The programme makes it possible to test for conflict between them and, where this occurs, the beliefs concerned undergo defensive transformation (equivalent to displacement, projection etc.). Such programmes are limited both by technological capacity and by the difficulty of making explicit the processes in question. Colby considers they may have value eventually in the training of analysts and also as a means of testing out the effect of different kinds of intervention by therapists. Computer models of particular individuals or kinds of individual might also eventually be more capable than a verbal description of representing the complex ways in which they are likely to react and process information. At the moment, the scope of such modelling is far more limited. It does have some value though in that devising appropriate programmes requires making explicit the processes and assumptions underlying the psychoanalytic concepts concerned.

The other approach is to consider how far the psychoanalytic theory of the mind is consistent with what we know about the functioning of the brain. Psychoanalysis, as we have seen, can be regarded as a method of therapy, a way of looking at actions and experiences, and as a set of propositions about how and why we behave and feel as we do. Underpinning all of these is a set of assumptions about the way the human mind works – a model of human nature – sometimes called the 'metapsychology' of psychoanalysis. It conceives of the mind essentially as a self-regulating organization – a perceptual system premised on biological drives and devoted to reducing the tensions arising from these. It operates through the interplay of forces designated as *id, ego* and *superego*, each creating tensions and governed by criteria of a different kind. Although not specifically described as such, the major features of this model of the mind have been made evident in the account of Freud's theories in Part One.

Freud began his career as a neurophysiologist. In 1895, he was inspired to delineate a possible neurological basis for his model of the mind. This complex and detailed work, the *Project for a Scientific Psychology*, was never published in his lifetime. In it, Freud offers a neurobiological account for key psychoanalytical concepts, including drives, cathexis, the ego, consciousness, reality-testing and defence. He expressed enormous enthusiasm while working on the *Project*. In a letter to his friend Fliess, he wrote:

> One evening last week when I was hard at work, tormented with just that amount of pain that seems to be the best state to make my brain function, the barriers were suddenly lifted, the veil was drawn aside, and I had a clear vision from the details of the neuroses to the conditions that make consciousness possible. Everything seemed to connect up, the whole worked well together, and one had the impression that the thing was now really a machine and would soon go by itself . . . I don't know how to contain myself for pleasure.[75]

Later, he gave up the work, calling it 'a kind of aberration'. He never again attempted explicitly to formulate a physiological basis for his theory.

More recently, commentators have begun to see in the *Project* a major influence on Freud's thought.[76] Pribram and Gill,[77] in particular, have argued that Freud's metapsychology is not a mere speculative model but is based on a sophisticated understanding of the workings of the brain as they were then known. They argue that, while 'the formulations of memory-motive mechanisms, attention, consciousness, and thought processes are as sophisticated as any available elsewhere and should therefore become part of the heritage of academic cognitive psychology', Freud's metapsychology can be usefully modified in the light of more recent neurophysiological research. They point out, for example, how Freud's conceptualization of unconscious and conscious processes might be linked to findings like those of Sperry[78] that the two hemispheres of the brain seem to operate in rather different ways.

> Eccles (1970)[79] has interpreted these data to suggest that only the state regulated with the left, language producing, hemisphere should be termed 'conscious' and that the non-linguistic hemisphere is responsible for unconscious processes, while Sperry emphasizes, on the basis of non-linguistic behavioural indicators, the separate 'consciousness' of each.[80]

Pribram and Gill are not suggesting that psychoanalytic theory can ever be *reduced* to physiological explanation but rather that, as the two approaches (to use Donald Hebb's phrase) 'chart the shores of the same bay', they may be usefully compared. The *Project* they regard as 'a Rosetta stone for those interested in making communication between these realms of discourse possible.' How far it is possible to reconcile the two realms and how far they will always remain 'different levels of inquiry and explanation, one in the universe of meaning and the other in the universe of natural science'[81] is an issue on which the two authors of the book disagree. The problems which can arise from *confusion* of these levels is a topic taken up in the next chapter.

This review of supporting evidence has so far been entirely focused on psychoanalysis as theory. But what about its effectiveness as a method of therapy? It might be thought that, as the proof of the psychoanalytic pudding lies in its eating, this question carries important theoretical implications. But therapeutic success should by no means be taken as a measure of the validity of the theory. For, if beneficial change does come about with psychoanalysis, it does not follow that this is necessarily for the reason the analyst assumes. Perhaps it was merely that having someone to talk to in such an intimate way restored the patient's self-confidence, and it would not have mattered very much what the analyst did provided he offered a listening ear. Conversely, if a cure is not forthcoming, this does not mean that the therapist's analysis of the origins of the patient's condition was necessarily at fault. It may just be that conveying this interpretation to him was not in itself sufficient to bring about the change desired.

Nevertheless, the issue is of practical concern. Can we be sure that if we go to a psychoanalyst it will be a worthwhile experience? Are we likely to derive some benefit from doing so or possibly even end up worse than before? Freud himself was sceptical about the value of objective assessments of psychoanalytic therapy. In the *New Introductory*

Lectures, he reacted to a review by the Berlin Psychoanalytic Institute of the results of treatment by its members with the comment, 'statistics of that kind are in general uninstructive; the material worked upon is so heterogeneous that only very large numbers would show anything. It is wiser to examine one's individual experiences'.[x2] Most psychoanalysts have followed Freud in relying on their own experience for assurance that their therapy works. But, as pointed out earlier, an analyst's training and professional involvement is likely to make it difficult for him to seriously doubt this. So a prospective patient may well be inclined to look elsewhere for evidence to justify their confident attitude.

We might suppose that Freud's own 'individual experiences' would be well documented in his published case histories. What is perhaps surprising is that, in a lifetime's work, Freud reports on so few patients in any detail. In all of his published work, only twelve cases are discussed in depth and in some of these the details given are far from complete.[x3] As Fisher and Greenberg[x4] have pointed out, of these, the outcome of only one – Paul Lorenz, the Rat Man – could be considered an unqualified success. When we bear in mind that the cases published were quite probably selected for their exemplary nature, and also that Freud wrote them up from memory, it may well be felt that they hardly in themselves constitute grounds for faith in the benefits of psychoanalytic therapy.

In recent years, numerous investigations have tried to rectify this situation and assess just what the effects of psychoanalytic therapy are. They confront though a methodological minefield through which few, if any, have passed unscathed. First, there is the problem of actually finding unequivocal and comparable examples of Freudian psycho-analytic therapy to evaluate. In practice, there is clearly considerable variation in what psychoanalysts who call themselves Freudian do. Although most still focus on the analysis of transference, they can differ quite widely on the length and goals of their treatment and in the ways in which they interact with the patient (e.g. how far they are directive or actively intervene). Some surveys[x5] imply that just about the only thing they have in common is a couch and a 55 minute hour. And these days some do not even use a couch! Like other professionals, individual analysts vary too in how good they are at their job. Characteristics such as warmth and capacity for empathy have also been shown to be signifi-cantly related to how effective a therapist is.[x6] It is clear, therefore, that a researcher needs to use a substantive sample if he is to be sure that the results he observes are due to psychoanalytic methods and are not just a function of the qualities of the analyst him or herself.

Even supposing our investigator finds his sample – several analysts who consistently use a similar Freudian approach – then he still has to find a way of measuring to what extent their patients improve. Several methods have been tried – psychoanalysts' assessments of any change that has occurred, evaluations by the patients' themselves or by others who know them well, and behavioural criteria such as incidence of subsequent hospitalization. But each in its own way is far from satisfactory.

Even if he can be sure that positive change *has* come about and that it is not due to the personal qualities of a particular therapist, it is still difficult to attribute it with certainty to the psychoanalytic treatment *per se*. One alternative has already been mooted. A patient will receive from his analyst a degree of uncritical interest and attention that he is unlikely ever to have bestowed on him elsewhere. It would not be surprising if this in itself could precipitate change. Then there is the possibility that patients can get better anyway quite regardless of treatment. The ministrations of friends and family, the experience of living, just the passing of time, may all have beneficial effects. Eysenck has argued that, to prove itself, psychotherapy must be able to demonstrate better results than could occur merely due to such *spontaneous remission* of symptoms. He worked out that a 70% success rate could be expected as a result of spontaneous remission alone, whereas the success rate for psychoanalysis was only 44% (66% if patients withdrawing before completion of treatment are ignored).[87] On these estimations, psychoanalysis as therapy must be regarded as, if anything, worse than useless. However, both Eysenck's figures and conclusions have been hotly challenged.[88] It is worth looking at the controversy in a little detail as it brings out the nature of some of the problems bedevilling the topic. Eysenck based his estimates of spontaneous remission on extensive but rather crude data from two American surveys. The first[89] noted how many neurotic patients in a hospital where they had received no specific treatment other than care, had nevertheless been discharged from hospital as improved. The other was a survey of people making insurance claims for neurotic complaints.[90] Those who, after seeing only their normal doctor, were able to go back to work or dropped their claims within two years were taken as examples of 'spontaneous cures'. Eysenck's critics have made a number of telling points. For example, there is no reason to assume that the patients in these surveys are sufficiently similar to those undergoing psychoanalysis to allow effective comparisons to be made. Nor is there any reason to assume that the criteria for discharge in any way resembled what a psychoanalyst would assess as 'improvement'. Eysenck's estimates for the success rate of psychoanalysis was based on his classification of patients' outcomes in case-studies published by analysts. But doubt has been cast on his interpretations of these and Rosenzweig[91] has claimed that in one instance (a paper by Fenichel) Eysenck even miscounted the number of cases reported. Other estimations of the success rate of psychoanalysis have been substantially higher.[92] And more recent studies of improvement without treatment have produced highly variable results though almost always lower than Eysenck's figure. Bergin's review[92], for example, found estimates ranging from 0% to 46%. It is clear that we should be very wary of accepting Eysenck's arguments and conclusions at their face value.

Instead of dubious estimates of spontaneous remission as a baseline, another approach is to use control and comparison groups. Ideally, this involves setting up comparable groups of patients, either by assigning them at random or by ensuring that those in each group have a similar range of characteristics. The patients in each group would then undergo psychoanalysis, some other type of psychotherapy or no treatment at all. Again, this is more easily said than done. Problems of assessment make effective matching of patients difficult. There are also ethical difficulties in the use of control groups in situations like this in that it may mean withholding treatment from a person which he feels he needs. Results of patients already having different kinds of psychotherapy could be compared. But this would be complicated by the possibility that different types of patients might be drawn to select particular psychotherapies. We could never be sure the comparison groups were comparable to start with.

Given this methodological obstacle race, it is not surprising that Kline, after reviewing work in the area, should conclude that 'studies of the outcome of psychoanalytic therapy where even the minimum standards of methodology, using control groups and quantification of results, are satisfied, simply do not exist.'[93]

Nevertheless, there are several studies which have been carried out with care, including some by analysts assessing their own results.[94] Even though a range of measures have been used including therapist and patient evaluations and test results, the findings consistently indicate that psychoanalysis is, for the majority of patients, preferable to no treatment at all. This though is very much what has emerged also from studies of other forms of psychotherapy, and what comparisons have been done (for example between psychoanalysis and Rogerian nondirective therapy) suggest that, in terms of effectiveness, there is little to choose between them.[95]

Kline has argued that there are better ways than such general assessments to determine the efficacy of psychoanalytic treatment. As an example, he cites the pioneering work of Bellak[96] who found that psychoanalysts listening to a recording of a therapeutic session were able to predict fairly well what would happen on the next occasion. This method has the advantage of obviating the need both for control groups and for assessment of change. However, there is no guarantee that ability to predict what will happen is related to the improvement of patients.

The very predictability of the sessions may merely reflect the possibility that the therapist is subtly manipulating the patient. Certainly though, alternatives to general assessment are called for. We need to look more precisely than has as yet proved possible at just what psychoanalysis does and why. It may well be, as Kline has suggested, that psychoanalysis is valuable as a diagnostic tool but that behaviour therapy and desensitization based on conditioning techniques can often be more effective in changing behaviours. Perhaps the most effective therapy will involve mixing different approaches.

Bannister[97] has also argued, though from a rather different standpoint, that research 'should be concerned with the issue of *what is going on in psychotherapy*'. He sees resort to questions like 'is psychotherapy effective?' as yet another example of the unfortunate influence of the medical model on psychological affairs. Psychotherapy should not be thought of as equivalent to the physical treatment of disease. It has sufficient moral justification in itself, he argues, in that it involves one person *paying heed* to another. It is as pointless to ask about its general effectiveness as it would be to ask 'is conversation effective?'

Bannister's points do stimulate us to stop to think about what psychoanalytic therapy really is. Perhaps it is best regarded, not as therapy, but as a form of personal education. Like any other education, its aim is to help us to think in a more detailed or differentiated way. It draws our attention to aspects of ourselves of which we may have hitherto been unaware and shows us new ways of making sense of ourselves and our relationships. We can try these out for size – to see if they work for us. But, like any form of understanding, these interpretations can never be regarded as the final word. They are always open to revision and change as we experience new events and alternative constructions become possible. Seen in this way, it is not surprising that psychoanalysis often takes the interminable time it does. It also perhaps casts a rather different light on the process of patient selection. Psychoanalysts are often accused of being over-discriminating in choosing who they will take on as patients. But, as with a difficult educational course, certain abilities and motivations may well be crucial in determining the benefits a patient may obtain.

How far such an educational process is likely to reduce anxiety or depression, generate behavioural change or a greater sense of fulfilment in life is another question. It seems probable that this will vary greatly depending on the patient and his initial state. There is no necessary connection and these are certainly not the only, if indeed the key, criteria which should be used in evaluating its worth.

In this context, it is interesting to consider how Freud's views about his own therapy changed during his lifetime. Beginning as a neurologist, he approached his work from a medical standpoint. Patients were seen as ill and his job was to cure them. In these years he had high confidence in the power of psychoanalysis as a therapy and he saw this rather than theory as its primary value. But Freud was far too good a scientist to ignore his experience. Later, while he still believed it to be the best form of psychotherapy available for the problems with which he dealt, he began to acknowledge its limitations. In the *New Introductory Lectures* he drily noted 'I do not think our cures can compete with those of Lourdes', and later in the same lecture, '. . . psychoanalysis began as a method of treatment; but I did not want to commend it to your interest as a method of treatment but on account of truths it contains, on account of the information it gives us about what concerns human beings most of all – their own nature – and on account of the connections it discloses between the most different of their activities.'[98]

On one hand, this gradual realization of the relative impotence of psychoanalysis (as of any psychotherapy) to change people may be taken as an acknowledgement of its failure so far to develop techniques to render its capacity for diagnosis into the power to cure. On the other, it can be taken to imply something about the very nature of psychoanalysis and its subject-matter themselves. In the last quotation Freud reveals his personal predilection for the power of insight rather than of cure. And, for him, psychoanalysis retains this capacity even if its ability to 'improve' people is open to doubt. By implication, at least, Freud now seems himself to acknowledge that the role of the psychoanalyst is essentially that of educator – a seeker and stimulator of insights – rather than begetter of cures. The distinction between the two is an important one both for practice and theory. It echoes a division made a few pages back between the universe of *meaning* and that of *medicine and natural science*. As will be argued shortly when the issue is discussed in greater depth, the failure to discriminate between them has been a major source of confusion in Freud's ideas and has served to mislead both analysts and evaluators of their work.

Looking back over the studies mentioned in the preceding pages, it is hard not to be impressed by the ingenuity which so many researchers have shown in testing psychoanalytic ideas. It is perhaps surprising how much support has been forthcoming. Some specific propositions have not been confirmed but, all in all, the results have been reasonably consistent with what the theory might predict. And yet you might be excused for wondering what all this research really adds. In comparison with the natural sciences, we are left with little sense of defined progress. Several studies have failed to replicate the findings of others. The measures used seem often to be only capable of tapping in a crude and superficial way the subtlety of Freud's ideas. And, apart from a few suggestions for minor modifications, this mass of research has not generated, as one might expect, any real creative development of the theory. True – there is evidence which is often consistent or suggestive but hardly, if ever, does it provide a *definitive* basis for rejecting or supporting specific ideas. Why should this be so?

One reason lies in the nature of the concepts and propositions which psychoanalysis employs. A central requirement for scientific testing is that, in some way, the propositions of a theory can be precisely related to observable consequences. A key problem with psychoanalysis is that its concepts are very often not grounded in observables but are defined in terms of other hypothetical concepts proposed by the theory. Repression, for example, can only really be defined by reference to *id, ego, superego*, and the concept of the unconscious. Even where specific hypotheses are more explicit than this, because they are likely to concern the *meaning* of an action or experience, they are not easy to test in a way which excludes other possible interpretations of the results. We have seen numerous examples of this problem. Hall's discovery of sex differences in the content of dreams and Friedman's observations of differences between boys and girls in their reactions to projective pictures and stories, which both investigators see as consistent with the Oedipus idea, *could* be explicable in terms of sex role socialization. Farrell[99] also uses the problem of validating the Oedipus complex as an example of the difficulty of finding related observations which permit unequivocal interpretation. The sexual attraction a boy experiences towards his mother at between the age of about three to five and his jealousy of his father might be presumed to express themselves in observable behaviours like climbing into bed beside his mother and pushing father away. But such actions are equally open to the interpretation that a psychoanalyst in the Adlerian tradition might give them – that they represent an expression of the child's wish to compensate for the feelings of inferiority he feels in relation to his father. So, even if we observe such behaviours, we cannot take them as an unequivocal demonstration of Oedipal dynamics.

A second kind of problem is that psychoanalytic propositions are almost always couched in probabilistic terms – they predict what is *likely* to happen rather than what definitely will. So strict toilet training will *tend* to lead to later anal characteristics but there is no guarantee these will result. There will always be children who, because of their constitution, will remain relatively immune. A related aspect is that psychoanalytically defined attributes very often have more than one manifestation. Anal character can show itself as stinginess or creativity; the presence of an unconscious desire may express itself directly or, because of the operation of defence mechanisms, only in partial form or even in actions of a totally unrelated kind. Conversely, very different, even opposite determinants may give rise to similar behaviours. Fixation, for example, can arise from both deprivation and overindulgence. This variability between determinant and effect makes it extremely difficult, if not impossible, to decisively refute psychoanalytic propositions. Strictly speaking, they are *unfalsifiable*. As Alasdair MacIntyre has put it 'the hypothesis has become a bet that cannot lose; but by the same token, as Karl Popper has shown, it cannot win. Whatever the behaviour, the hypothesis is not falsified and its unfalsifiability is fatal to its status as a hypothesis.'[100]

Because of such characteristics and the consequent difficulty of obtaining *definitive* experimental support for psychoanalytic theory, some critics have been tempted to dismiss it as of little scientific value – as having no more claim than 'Homer's collected stories from Olympus'[101] or as a paradigm which has outlived what usefulness it may have had.[102] But any evaluation, like any theory, is a construction. It reflects the values and assumptions of the evaluator. For a philosopher like Popper who considers falsifiability as the key to progress in science, and for an experimental psychologist like Eysenck, testability is the essential basis for scientific development. A *scientific* theory is one which yields hypotheses which are potentially refutable by empirical test.

But is a theory which does not live up to this criterion scientifically valueless? Scientific progress depends on more than just checking how well hypotheses fit. It requires creation as well as evaluation. No other psychological theory stands comparison with psychoanalysis in the breadth and richness of the ideas and interpretations it yields.

It is also arguable as to how far psychoanalysis should be considered untestable. It is true that its propositions are difficult to refute. Nevertheless, it is still possible to bring the weight of evidence to bear and to see how far it is consistent with the suggestions that the theory makes. This at least provides a rational basis for deciding whether a given idea is tenable or not. It was in this way that Freud was able to develop his theory, modifying it in the light of how well it worked. In any instance of this kind, the fit may be a little loose. An alternative *ad hoc* hypothesis may hold up equally well. But what is impressive about psychoanalysis and an achievement which no other single theory can sustain, is the range of situations for which the theory can give a plausible account.

As Farrell[103] has argued, psychoanalysis, for all its empirical and logical indeterminacy, is not untypical of ideas which have had considerable importance and influence in the history of science. He compares it with Isaac Newton's theory of cohesion which 'was not open to validation, was untestable and vacuous' and yet played 'a significant role in the subsequent history of scientific inquiry into the nature of chemical reactions and matter'.[104] Psychoanalysis has not only had a profound influence on the approach and methods used by professionals like social workers and psychiatrists who are concerned with the care and emotional welfare of others, but, like Newton's theory of cohesion, has served a vital heuristic function. It has stimulated an enormous amount of thought and research about the nature of the human condition.

Finally, and most importantly perhaps, it is disputable as to whether the essence of science lies in adherence to a particular kind of method (i.e., quantification and experiment) which has proved so successful in the natural sciences, or whether it is in rational and systematic investigation of whatever kind is best likely to yield understanding of the subject matter in question. It is noteworthy that not only psychoanalysis but research in other human sciences like anthropology, psychiatry and much of social psychology is also open to similar methodological criticism. This raises the question as to whether the complexities of subtleties of mental life just may not be reducible to propositions which are clearly definable, operational and permit clear-cut refutation without significant impairment of their essential qualities. It is a question of emphasis. You may restrict yourself to the rigorously testable and, in so doing, inevitably ignore the subtlety and the more intangible aspects of behaviour and experience. Or you may choose, as Freud did, to tackle complexity head on in as sytematic a fashion as possible and try to make sense of it even though the concepts you are forced to employ may be 'woolly' and your propositions not easily refutable.

CHAPTER 11

The Significance of Meaning

What is it about mental life which makes it so intractable a subject-matter? I would like to suggest that the problems arise because its essence is *meaning*. This is an idea which has been hinted at earlier, in the discussion of therapy as education rather than as cure; Pribram and Gill's comments on Freud's *Project* also raised the notion of natural science and human meaning as fundamentally different realms of discourse. By referring to the essence of mental life as meaning, I am pointing to the fact that the conduct of our lives and relationships is ordered by concepts. The ways we conceptualize and feel about ourselves, other people or a situation will be fundamental to the ways we behave. In everyday life, we take this for granted. There are occasions when we explain behaviours by reference to causes. We were late because of the traffic. Or we attribute bad conduct to the effects of drink. More often though we assume we are the *agents* of our actions. For our explanations of behaviour in this case we resort not to causes but to reasons premised on beliefs and feelings. He got angry because she considered he had behaved badly. She signed the petition because she believed it might do some good. He did not go on holiday because he preferred to save the money instead. A critical difference about explanations of this kind is that they are open to negotiation. He might well be able to assuage her anger if he can convince her that what he did was with good intent. She can be persuaded not to sign the petition if we can get her to realize that it may do more harm than good. And, by pointing out the present rate of inflation, we might well be able to undermine his desire to save. A good deal of our everyday interactions are concerned with negotiating the meanings of action. We are continuously testing and modifying our interpretations either *explicitly* by exchanging views with others or *implicitly* by noting their example of ways of interpreting events. One way of viewing a psychotherapy session is as a negotiation of this kind. It may not involve direct persuasion but the patient is likely to be encouraged to revise the way he construes himself and his relationships. Thus psychotherapy is quite distinct from physical medicine. Its core is the manipulation of meaning not of body functioning.

Already we can see that meaning as subject-matter is a slippery and amoeba-like customer with which to deal. As soon as we grasp it, it can change its shape. And there is worse in store. Meanings, like theories and evaluations, are constructions. The form they take depends upon the perspective from which they are viewed. The meaning of the same situation may be read in different ways. An action which one person thinks is cowardly another may see as circumspect. What a monarchist may consider to be loyal pride an analyst may interpret as transference. So we get the curious possibility of a theoretically infinite array of meanings possible for any situation we choose to explore. Fortunately though perhaps, meanings are unlikely to be entirely private or personal. They exist as part of complex, interrelated social systems of construing arising out of shared experience. In practice, the meanings we apply to any one situation are limited by the need to fit them within the categories provided by a system of this kind. Even given this though, there are still likely to be quite a few alternative ways of making sense of the same action or event.

Not just different perspectives but different *levels* of meaning can co-exist. The meaning of an action, for example, at one level may arise from the function it serves. In this respect, it is likely to be universal to all people. Over and above this, it may carry a meaning derived from its symbolic significance in a particular culture or group. This aspect of meaning is likely to be confined to those who have shared its usage in this way. Psychoanalysis alerts us to the further possibility that beyond this again, it may carry meaning of which even the actor is unaware.

> We'd go over one of the black-humoured incidents that kept our spirits up on the long death march when we'd come out of Auschwitz and the Germans were trying literally to walk us to death before the war ended. You weren't allowed to stop and, excuse me, relieve yourself whenever you needed; you'd wait until your guards stopped and gave permission for all to perform. Then a group of perhaps ten of us, all Auschwitz girls, would quite deliberately form a line, lift up our skirts and turn our bare bottoms rudely to the Germans. [1]

What was a functional need was turned to good use and transformed into a symbolic insult. Presumably this meaning was not registered by the guards. Otherwise, it would have invited their retaliation. So here, we may suppose, is a gesture which is interpreted at different levels by those involved. But there may also be another level of meaning which was hidden from them all. Like many insulting gestures, it has a sexual association. The gesture is not unlike the behaviour of females of other primate species when presenting sexually. A psychoanalyst or an ethologist might well be tempted to read into it the possibility of an unconscious expression of this kind, one which at a conscious level would have been utterly denied by the girls themselves. There is no way of validating whether or not this is the case, except perhaps to look for other aspects of behaviour consistent with the idea. But nevertheless it is a meaning which *could* be assigned.

If we accept that meanings lie at the heart of mental life, and that meaning has the kind of characteristics described above, then it may well seem that a science of mental life devoted to the search through experiment for universal laws is a largely irrelevant pursuit. For the meanings underlying actions are flexible and negotiable. They are individual and dependent on specific historical circumstance. They are not marshallable into immutable cause–effect laws that apply across time and cultures. Rather than such a nomothetic approach, what is needed (at least in the first stage of the development of the discipline) is an idiographic one. The task becomes the detailed exploration of patterns of meaning implicit in actions or events. The goal is to make these as explicit as possible. How and why have they come about? How do they fit in with the wider context in which they occur.

This kind of distinction is not new. It originates in a controversy dating back to the early Greeks. Do the phenomena of the mind differ fundamentally from those of matter? Several social scientists have argued that they do. Wilhelm Dilthey, among others, has pointed out the difference between the kind of knowing possible for the world of objects (*Wissen*) and that of human experience and psychological concerns (*Verstehen*). While the former includes observation and measurements, the latter is inevitably dependent on introspection and interpretation and is essentially qualitative in form. Interestingly, Freud made a similar differentiation in the *Project*, when discussing the interface between brain and mind: 'Our consciousness furnishes only *qualities*, whereas (physical) science recognises only *quantities* . . . it is to be expected from the structure of the nervous system that it consists of contrivances for transforming external quantity into quality.'[2]

The analysis above then is questioning the appropriateness of applying a natural science paradigm to the study of mental life. For a genuinely *psychological science*, what is needed is a *hermeneutic* approach. This likens the analysis of actions and experience to the interpretative study of a text. Different languages code and encapsulate meanings in different ways. The art of hermeneutics is to extract the meaning a particular text may hold. This involves not only knowing the implications of the symbols used but of their significances in relation to each other and the context in which they appear. Like a text, actions and experiences may be regarded as encoded meanings. They are not objective facts but take their significance from the meanings they convey. These arise through shared usage. Socialization just as much involves learning the meanings of actions through interacting with other people as it does learning a spoken language which captures meanings in patterns of sound.

The analogy with language is a useful one. As meaning is transformed into speech so too it is into actions. Their form depends on conventions which have to be learned. They depend too on an underlying syntax or set of rules. Meaning is generated into surface forms and inferred from these by means of a knowledge (albeit implicit) of such rules.

In everyday life, we do marvellously well in interpreting the speech and actions of others and conveying meanings to them. Quite often indeed we may even communicate quite unwittingly ('give off' to use Goffman's term) what we would prefer to keep concealed. But not all meanings are easily open to access. They may remain implicit and hidden even from ourselves. It was Freud's achievement to realize this. The unconscious generates its meanings too. But, as Lacan[3] has pointed out, this is a language which we have to learn. The particular contribution of Freud was to provide a 'depth hermeneutics' to help us penetrate its particular codes and rules. This view of psychoanalysis appealed to Freud himself. He draws a similar analogy in *The Interpretation of Dreams*.

> The dream-thoughts and the dream-content are presented to us like two versions of the same subject-matter in two different languages. Or, more properly, the dream-content seems like a transcript of the dream-thoughts into another mode of expression, whose characters and syntactic laws it is our business to discover by comparing the original and the translation. The dream-thoughts are immediately comprehensible, as soon as we have learnt them. The dream-content, on the other hand, is expressed as it were in a pictographic script, the characters of which have to be transposed individually into the language of the dream-thoughts. If we attempted to read these characters according to their pictorial value instead of according to their symbolic relation, we should clearly be led into error. Suppose I have a picture-puzzle, a rebus, in front of me. It depicts a house with a boat on its roof, a single letter of the alphabet, the figure of a running man whose head has been conjured away, and so on. Now I might be misled into raising objections and declaring that the picture as a whole and its component parts are nonsensical. A boat has no business to be on the roof of a house, and a headless man cannot run. Moreover, the man is bigger than the house; and if the whole picture is intended to represent a landscape, letters of the alphabet are out of place in it since such objects do not occur in nature. But obviously we can only form a proper judgement of the rebus if we put aside criticisms such as these of the whole composition and its parts

and if, instead, we try to replace each separate element by a syllable or word that can be represented by that element in some way or other. The words which are put together in this way are no longer nonsensical but may form a poetical phrase of the greatest beauty and significance. A dream is a picture-puzzle of this sort and our predecessors in the field of dream-interpretation have made the mistake of treating the rebus as a pictorial composition: and as such it has seemed to them nonsensical and worthless.[4]

As was argued in Chapter 9, the strength of psychoanalysis lies in its semantic value – in other words, its extension of our hermeneutic power. Freud helps us to penetrate the meaning not only of dreams but of mistaken actions, the effects of jokes, and the transformations which meanings undergo in neurosis. His own writings are full of tenaciously worked-out examples ranging from speculations about why he happened to misplace a particular book to a study of personal significances in Dostoevsky's novels.

When regarded as a hermeneutic method, psychoanalysis' weakness as an experimental science becomes its very strength. Take the idea of *over-determination*. In discussing the condensation which occurs in dreams, it was pointed out that many different strands of meaning may underlie a single remembered image or event. Psychoanalytic interpretation is aimed at unravelling these. Moreover, the concepts the theory provides help us to view the meanings from different perspectives and levels. Concepts like 'mechanisms of defence', for example, serve to relate consciously-registered meanings to those operative at an unconscious level. Although this makes it impossible to submit any interpretation to precise test, it does offer great potential for putting together the detailed picture of all the different meanings which may be involved. As Munroe has put it:

> Freud does not extrapolate human behaviour from a few general principles, handling complications by purely logical deduction roughly checked against experience. On the contrary, he has introduced a whole series of concepts which order observations at different levels, from different angles. This *multidimensionality* is somewhat confusing and I think the Freudians themselves often get tangled up in it. Nevertheless, I feel so very strongly about its positive value for psychological science that I should like to state here . . . that it is the main strength of the Freudian position.[5]

This capacity of psychoanalysis to view observations from different perspectives is also shown by its concern not just with meaning itself in all its forms but with the significance of the *distortions* which that meaning may have undergone. Why has it been transformed in that particular fashion? Here the analyst becomes a historian or an archeologist, trying to reconstruct the sequence of experiences which over time have created the need to disguise disturbing feelings in certain ways. As Freud was well aware, the act of interpretation itself is also open to such systematic bias. A purpose of training analysis was to alert the psychoanalyst to this and to give him some insight into the kind of defensive distortions he might be prey to. In this sense, as Habermas[6] has pointed out, 'psycho-analysis is . . . the only tangible example of a science incorporating methodological self-reflection.'[7]

Psychoanalysis has a reflexive character in another sense. If we accept that meanings are the essence of our actions and experience, then one extraordinary consequence is the power of a psychological theory to change the nature of the subject-matter it is theorizing about. Unlike the physical sciences, the subjects of its study are capable of awareness of the explanations put forward about them. This awareness may lead to change in the beliefs which people have about themselves and others and hence the basis on which we assume their actions to depend. (There is a somewhat similar effect in physics – the Heisenberg uncertainty principle. This points out that the transmission of energy from an electron microscope necessary to observe the movement of atomic particles itself leads to movement of the particles, thus affecting the observations made. However, such observation effects are likely to be more specific and less variable than is the case with human subjects and the problem is far more pervasive in psychology.) A reflexive effect of this kind may be reactive – where people bloody-mindedly ensure that they behave in any way other than in that which the theory predicts. More likely though it will be self-fulfilling. Their assimilation of the conceptualization of themselves and their actions put forward by a theory becomes part of the basis for the way they behave. The kind of impact which psychoanalysis has in this respect is a topic which will be explored in Chapter 13.

Another curious feature of psychological meanings, which is perhaps emphasized in modern cultures, is their orientation to the future. Our awareness in the world is much concerned with consequence. It is our hopes and aspirations – what we want to bring about, as much as the way we think things are – that generates our behaviour. Our actions are constrained and shaped too by what we assume to be the right thing to do. This judgement may be premised on moral principles, a desire to please or not appear different, or simply on need for our own gratifica-tion. But, in the broadest sense, the meanings of our actions have a moral flavour in that they are concerned with intentions, with choice, with what is best for us to do. Given this and the potential influence of psychological theory on the way we live our lives, it may well be appro-priate to distinguish psychoanalysis (and also other fields of psycho-logical and social study) as a *moral* rather than a natural science.

Many commentators on Freud have failed to recognize that psycho-analysis, with meaning as its subject-matter, is a fundamentally different enterprise from a natural science. (They have not been helped by the tendency remarked on earlier for Freud's concepts to be rendered in English in a more abstract and quasi-scientific form.) They consider that its methodological difficulties may be attributed to its youthfulness as a discipline (though, as the age of sciences go, it should by now be quite ready to sprout a beard!) Or it is seen as a temporary stand-in until more respectable science can fill the gap. As Farrell asserts:

> If we accept the analogy with the history of general medicine, then it is reasonable to maintain that the development of psychiatry depends on the development of the sciences fundamental to it – namely, those concerned to unlock the neuro-chemical machinery of the nervous system. As and when this comes about, a psychiatrist *will* then come to know what is 'the matter with' mental patient Joe . . . Those of us who are rash may be ready to bet that analysis as *treatment* will be replaced by cheaper and more effective *physical* methods, which will affect the functioning of the biological machinery responsible for our inner world and outer behaviour.[8]

This reductionist view fails to acknowledge the fundamental distinction I have laboured to make above. The goal of hermeneutics is not so much to cure or even explain, as to raise consciousness; i.e., it is to generate awareness of self and the possible meanings which may underlie the ways we act or feel. No pill can ever achieve that on its own. The methodological flaws and lack of defined progress in orthodox scientific terms which appear to characterize psychoanalysis are not because it is an immature natural science. Rather they arise because they are intrinsic to the nature of the very different task it confronts.

The confusion between the two approaches is not confined to commentators on Freud. It is endemic in his own work. The first years of his career were spent in the laboratory and his first published papers were in neurophysiology. He never entirely discarded the rational materialism in which he was reared. Freud's ambition to be a great scientist always remained with him. It was the reactions of the medical journals to his *Interpretation of Dreams* which concerned him rather than the literary or philosophical reviews. His goal was still to establish the natural laws he assumed to govern the operation of the psyche. His model of the mind was couched in biological and physicalistic terms. He believed in the objective nature of his theory. To him it was natural science.

> You should not for a moment suppose that what I put before you as the psychoanalytic view is a speculative system. It is on the contrary empirical – either a direct expression of observations or the outcome of a process of working them over.[9]

Nevertheless, Freud was far too good a scientist to ignore what he found. Gradually his theory focused more on interpretation. And Freud was a consummate hermeneuticist. He is never happier than when in search of some hidden seam of meaning, assiduously sifting the evidence for the slightest clues. Cioffi highlights the nature of Freud's style. 'Symptoms, errors, etc. are not simply *caused by* but they "announce", "proclaim", "express", "realize", "fulfil", "gratify", "represent", "irritate" or "allude to" this or that repressed impulse thought, memory, etc.'[10] To Cioffi this is merely unscientific imprecision. We might recognize it rather as an implicit acknowledgement of the significance of qualitative meaning rather than of quantitative cause. But while his work becomes more hermeneutic in character and concerns itself in practice with the vagaries of meaning, he never really relinquishes his conviction that psychoanalysis is natural science.

The conflict shows through in his writings. In the same paper (*The Question of Lay Analysis*) in which he argues that psychoanalysis is *not* a medical and scientific speciality, he writes of interpretation as objective fact. 'When you have attained some degree of self-discipline and have certain knowledge at your disposal, your interpretations will be independent of your personal characteristics and will hit the mark.'[11] It shows too in the ambivalence of his attitude to his own work. His pretensions to science make it imperative for him to treat his theories as confirmed laws. In *Beyond the Pleasure Principle*, he describes his argument for the death instinct as 'speculation, often far-fetched speculation . . . an attempt to follow an idea consistently, out of curiosity to see where it will lead'.[12] And yet, shortly afterwards, with little more to support the idea, he writes as if it were an established reality. On other occasions though he clearly acknowledges the tentative and provisional nature of his conceptualizations. In *Beyond the Pleasure Principle* he wrote 'We must be ready, too, to abandon a path that we have followed for a time, if it seems to be leading to no good end'.[13] He used too the term 'mythology' to describe his theory. Freud reconciled these contrasting views by attributing the provisional quality of his theories to the difficulty of his task. If his ideas were scientifically suspect, they were still better than none at all. He quotes the lines of a poem, 'What we cannot reach flying, we must reach limping . . .'[14] Explicitly, he adhered to his empiricist position, never quite making the leap to open acknowledgement of the intrinsically hermeneutic nature of his work. His evaluation though at the conclusion of *An Autobiographical Study* seems realistic enough.

> Looking back, then, over the patchwork of my life's labours, I can say that I
> have made many beginnings and thrown out many suggestions. Something
> will come of them in the future, though I cannot myself tell whether it will

be much or little. I can, however, express a hope that I have opened up a pathway for an important advance in our knowledge.[15]

It could well be argued that Freud's ambivalence was justified in that it merely reflects the dual nature of actions and experience, rooted as they are in both biology and the symbolic. For the human adult, biological needs are mediated by symbolic forms. It is this, as we have seen, which gives them such enormous variability of expression and often inhibits their fulfilment. At the same time, we must suppose that these symbolic forms are themselves based on and constrained by the body and the development of its needs. Reason and cause, meaning and biology are intrinsically intertwined. Freud was concerned not just with the penetration of meaning but with the way the system which generates it works. If his explicit emphasis sometimes seems to fall upon the latter, it was because 'Mankind has always known that it possesses spirit; I had to show it that there are also instincts'.[16] Freud courageously confronted the dual nature of man. It was his strength not to seek refuge in a one-sided concentration on hermeneutics *or* natural science.

What then does psychoanalysis offer? Although it provides a model of the mind which is essentially *psychobiological*, it does not constitute a set of scientific laws. What it does yield is a set of interesting concepts which *can* be useful tools, a set of hypotheses which may alert us and sensitize us to consistencies and subtleties in the phenomena of mental life we encounter and thus, by their differentiating function, enrich our understanding and capacity to predict. Both theory and interpretations are invariably provisional and are developed by a system of continuous, progressive adjustment in the light of their consistency with available evidence. Such 'progressive approximations' demand sensitivity of perception, tolerance of ambiguity and great skill on the part of the analyst. Unlike much of academic psychology, in psychoanalysis the psychologist is not, in Henry Murray's phrase 'the forgotten tool of psychology'.

Whether or not you regard the product of Freud's labours as scientific depends on your view of science. There are those, like MacIntyre, who while acknowledging Freud's achievement in showing us 'hitherto unnoticed facts, hitherto unrevealed motives, hitherto unrelated facets of our lives'[17] are still reluctant to ascribe to this the status of science. 'As a discoverer he perhaps resembles a Proust or a Tolstoy rather than a Dalton or a Pasteur'.[18] There are others like Rieff[19] who, while acknowledging that psychoanalysis cannot match the rigid standards of scientific theory, is concerned;

. . . lest this label 'unscientific' be used to condemn Freud or, worse, to praise him condescendingly for just those rare qualities in him that we do not encourage among ourselves: his wide range and subtlety, his unsurpassed brilliance as an exegete of the universal language of pain and suffering, his willingness to pronounce judgments and draw out the evidence for them from his own life as well as from clinical data. His scientific motives are of a piece with the ethical implications of his thought, whose catch phrases have seeped down from the conversations of the educated into the popular consciousness of the age. It would be an impertinence, into which no received notion of the boundary between science and ethics should lead us, to judge one of Freud's faces authentic and dismiss the other. For humanists in science, and for scientists of the human, Freud should be the model of a concern with the distinctively human that is truly scientific.[20]

If your critical criterion for science is the generation of propositions which are falsifiable then clearly psychoanalysis is not a science. But if you mean by 'science' the systematic formulation of concepts and hypotheses based on careful and detailed observations, then I think the answer must be that it is. It is arguable too, whether there is any other approach likely to offer better potential for the prediction of people's actions in real-life settings. For Freud, albeit reluctantly, takes on the uncomfortable but important task of confronting the Janus face of humans as they are – both biological and existential beings.

CHAPTER 12

A Personal Creation

A point which has been made in the first chapter and touched on subsequently several times is that no theory is a mere passive, objective mirror of external reality. It is a construction which will reflect the values and characteristics of the theorist and quite probably the social and intellectual climate in which it was devised. It is particularly instructive to consider psychoanalysis from this perspective. As we have seen it is a generative theory, rich in content and difficult to evaluate empirically. And, as has been argued, Freud in creating it brought to bear all the diversity of his own intellectual and cultural awareness. It also has important roots in his own self-analysis. Furthermore, it is a theory which touches on 'central aspects of man's existence' and, as Erikson has pointed out, in theorizing of this kind 'we can only conceptualize what is relevant to us for personal, for conceptual and for historical reasons'.[1]

Any attempt to analyse a theory in terms of its personal and social origins is inevitably speculative. Like any other interpretation, the only way we have of validating it is to judge its consistency – how well it makes sense – as an intelligible pattern. But it can serve the function of a hermeneutic analysis and alert us to the possible factors which *may* have contributed to the creation and the nature of the theory. The enterprise is complicated by the broad and complex canvas which Freud's theory presents, also by the fact that our access to relevant background information is fragmentary and incomplete. But Freud does leave many clues about his most intimate of introspections in his letters and in the often courageously self-revelatory examples which he draws on in his writings. With their help it is possible to sketch something of the personal background from which his ideas emerged.

Several references have already been made to Freud's intellectual inheritance. Many of the core ingredients of his theory were part of the fabric of thought of the time – notions of the unconscious were current in philosophy and accounts of the nature and significance of sexual development in childhood had appeared in medical journals and books.

The development of Freud's interests and career seems ideally suited to the founder of a theory which serves so well to bridge the biological and existential aspects of man. After his university studies and six years of research in physiology, he was well acquainted with the work of Darwin and Fechner, one of the founders of experimental psychology. His supervisor Brücke, drawing on the new ideas of Helmholtz and others about the nature of energy, had developed a concept of the organism as a dynamic system involving the flow and transformations of energy. Fairly early in his career, Freud witnessed too the demonstrations of hypnosis by Charcot and Bernheim, which suggested the possibility of levels of mind not available to consciousness. Not only must his background in science have provided Freud with training in systematic investigation but it is likely also to have sown the seeds for his conceptualization of the mind as a dynamic energy system operative on several levels.

On the other side, as we have seen in looking at his life, Freud was well-versed in literature, languages, history, and anthropology and archeology. He had read deeply in both classical and contemporary philosophy. Even though in the *Autobiography* he specifically disclaimed having read Schopenhauer until after his own work was well advanced, he was likely to have been acquainted with his ideas as well as those of Nietzsche. His philosophy teacher Brentano had been one of the forerunners of phenomenological psychology and his theorizing about the 'intentional' nature of conscious experience (i.e., we are aware of our perceptions or desires only in relation to some object, we cannot just be aware or desire something *in vacuo*) had been based on careful introspection and logical analysis.

Freud's experience of therapy enabled him to observe the mental life of others in intimate detail. It also forced him to confront its complexity. While his scientific and logical mind could seek for links and patterns in the complex fabric of patients' lives, his grounding in languages and the arts may have enabled him to cope better with ambiguity and appreciate the subtlety and significance of meanings.

Freud's personality too had implications for his work. An intense desire for fame is evident from his earliest days. Not only may this have fuelled his labours but it may have encouraged his 'grand theorizing' – his search for a conception to encompass all manifestations of human behaviour and experience. It was a factor underlying his preference for a career in science – a profession where he might hope to achieve renown – rather than content himself with the more modest role of therapist. Freud's quiet nightmare was to end up in the second rank, that all he would achieve would be 'recognition as a forerunner whose failure had been inevitable'. His writings hint that he saw the roots of this desire to succeed in the repressed hostility towards his father which he was to discover in his self-analysis. In one of his last published letters, to Romain Rolland in 1937, he described a visit to the Acropolis the previous year when a curious sense of unreality suddenly afflicted him while looking out over Athens. He reasoned that his visit to Greece symbolized a sense of superiority over his father. This was something that his father would never have been able to do nor would have appreciated if he had. The sense of unreality Freud interpreted as a defence against the unconscious guilt that this idea aroused. 'It seems as though the essence of success were to have got further than one's father, and as though to excel one's father were still something forbidden.'[2] But even as a child Freud must have seemed destined for greatness. He was born in a caul (i.e., with part of the foetal membrane still attached to his head) which was generally taken as an omen of good fortune. Jones[3] records several other family anecdotes about events which also augured later fame. For example, an old woman his mother met by chance in a shop when he was a child had prophesied a great future for him. Confidence too came, as we noted earlier, from having been his mother's favourite. He himself emphasized the value of this relationship: 'If a man has been his mother's undisputed darling he retains throughout life the triumphant feeling, the confidence in success which not seldom brings about success.'[4] It was only this sense of self-confidence, he reflected, which sustained him during the years of his 'splendid isolation' – a time when, as he believed, there was only opposition to his views. The experience of being Jewish he saw as having helped too by familiarizing him 'with the fate of being in the opposition', and thus laying the foundation for a 'degree of independence of judgement'.[5] Sulloway[6] has suggested though that Freud may have exaggerated the negativity of the reaction to his early work. Overcoming hardship is an intrinsic feature of the archetypal image of the hero. And it was as *conquistador* or an adventurer exploring the unknown hinterlands of the mind that he most liked to describe himself rather than as a scientist or thinker.

There is no record of the way in which Freud was brought up. What we know of him as a person though suggests quite marked anal tendencies. He was stubborn and although he does not appear to have been particularly mean, he certainly took great pride in what he produced. There are hints too of compulsive behaviour. Freud would often arrive at a station hours before the time of departure for fear of missing his train. He has also been accused of having a sadistic side. Roazen in his book *Brother Animal*[7] has dissected his relationship with a talented disciple Victor Tausk. He suggests that, due to resentment at the originality of Tausk's ideas which often threatened to anticipate his own, Freud deliberately humiliated the younger man. He refused his earnest request to be allowed to enter analysis with Freud, referring him instead to his student Helene

Deutsch. Shortly afterwards, Tausk shot and hanged himself. He had faced problems over both money and relationships but Roazen considers that Freud's coldness towards him had been a factor leading to his death.

What particularly concerns us here is to see in what ways the specific content of Freud's theory relates to the pattern of his life. One possibility, for example, is that his reliance on introspection may have led him to overemphasize the importance of repression and of sexual life. We noted earlier Jones' observation that Freud had strong emotions but even more powerful repressions. Inner conflict and transformation of libido prob- ably played a very real part in the dynamics of his own personality. Gillie[8] has suggested that a secret affair with his sister-in-law Minna may have had some influence on his theorizing. Apparently she bore some resemblance to his mother which may well have emphasized to Freud the possibility of incestuous feelings. The need to disguise his affection may also have served to throw into relief the way small slips of the tongue and actions can unwittingly reveal hidden feelings.

Drawing on biographical material and Freud's own references to his past, Stolorow and Atwood[9] have made a thought-provoking attempt to see his theory 'in the light of the subjective concerns which dominated his personal existence'.[10] Specifically they have tried to relate aspects of Freud's early experience to both his relationships as an adult and to his ideas on psychosexual development. A feature of Freud's childhood, they claim, was the theme of 'disappearing persons'. When he was only nineteen months old, his younger brother Julius died. At the age of three and at the time of the birth of his sister Anna, the Catholic Nanny who had brought him up was suddenly sent away. His adult half-brother Philipp had accused her of stealing and she was arrested and committed to prison. You may remember too that his father had been married at least once before. There is no reason to suppose that little Sigmund knew much about this. But one might well surmise that some hint had been dropped. For the young Freud, mysterious disappearances of mother figures may well have seemed somehow associated with older males – prescients perhaps of the Oedipus theme. Moreover, the loss of two of the most significant people in his life – his brother Julius and his Nanny – were inextricably linked with his own feelings of jealousy and anger consequently upon the birth of a younger rival. In a letter to Fliess, Freud admits that he had greeted the birth of Julius '. . . with ill wishes and genuine childish jealousy . . .'[11] He reasons that 'his death left the germ of self-reproaches in me'.[12] Such events may well have aroused anxiety in the little boy over the seemingly magical powers of his feelings to effect his desires.

It seems probable that his mother too would have incurred his feelings of reproach. Her confinement to give birth to his rivals had taken her away from him. But concern may also have been aroused that his anger might repeat the effects it had seemed to have in the past. The scene is set for what Stolorow and Atwood regard as a central dynamic in Freud's personal life – his early need to deny any feelings of hostility towards his mother. They document their case with illustrative material from Freud's own accounts. One memory which Freud later reports as having haunted him seems to suggest a fear of losing her.

> . . . my mother was nowhere to be found: I was screaming my head off. My brother Philipp, twenty years older than me, was holding open a cupboard for me, and when I found that my mother was not inside it either, I began crying still more, till, looking slim and beautiful, she came in by the door.[13]

This incident happened when he was three, at the time of his Nanny's dismissal and the birth of his younger sister. In a detailed analysis of the incident in the *Psychopathology of Everyday Life*[14] Freud links his concern that his mother may be in the cupboard with his knowledge that his missing Nanny had been 'locked-up'. His mother's slenderness provides an additional reassurance that the pregnancy which had taken her away from him is now over.

Later, at the age of seven, he dreams of: '. . . my beloved mother, with a peculiarly peaceful, sleeping expression on her features, being carried into the room by two (or three) people with birds' beaks and laid upon the bed'.[15] In his own analysis of this dream, although he notes associations with death, he attributes his upset to the conflict aroused by the sexual desire for his mother which he assumes the dream to represent. Stolorow and Atwood disagree. They interpret the dream as a disguised expression of hostility towards his mother. Freud's own need to defend himself against awareness of such wishes, they consider, prevented his own interpretation acknowledging this. If we accept their point of view, then it is a nice example of the kind of interpretative bias which training analysis is intended to counteract.

Stolorow and Atwood go on to argue that the characteristic defence which Freud used to maintain the repression of his negative feelings towards his mother was *over-idealization*. It is true that the manifest form of his references to her are almost all in highly positive terms.' Altogether the most perfect, the most free ambivalence of all human relationships'[16] is how he described the bond between mother and son. The authors suggest that this influenced his relationships as an adult. His tendency to idealize was transferred first to his fiancée Martha and later to his friend and mentor Wilhelm Fliess. They quote the adulation in his letters to his future wife as an expression of his idealization need, '. . . how much the magic of your being expresses itself in your countenance and your body, how much there is visible in your appearance that reveals how sweet, generous, and reasonable you are . . .'[17] The darker, unconscious side showed through in the violence of his jealous feelings and perhaps also in his over-concern for the health of both his wife and friend. Stolorow and Atwood suggest that even Freud's choice of career may have been influenced by his desires and conflicts in relation to his mother. According to his own account, his decision to study medicine was prompted by hearing Goethe's essay on nature read aloud. As Jones has pointed out, this pictures nature as 'a beautiful and bountiful mother who allows her favourite children the privilege of exploring her secrets'.[18]

The part of Stolorow and Atwood's analysis most pertinent to this discussion is their assertion that 'these same mental operations left their stamp on aspects of his theory of psychosexual development'. They see this in the fact that the theory tends to locate the source of the difficulties and dangers of development within the child's own feelings. It is his sexual and aggressive needs which are considered to be at the root of his conflicts. This they regard in part as a reflection of Freud's defensive need to preserve an idealized image of his parents. Any blame is internalized, as it was in his later relationships with Martha and Fliess, and not attributed to them. They take up Tomkins'[19] suggestion that in the theory he handles his repressed hostility by displacing it. In his ideas about the psychosexual development of *girls* in contrast to boys, the unconscious hostility is given full rein. This thesis is illustrated from Freud's own account in his discussion of 'feminity' in his *New Introductory Lectures*.[20] In describing the shift in the little girl's affection from her mother to her father, for example, he writes:

> The turning away from the mother is accomplished by hostility; the attachment to the mother ends in hate. A hate of that kind may become very striking and last all through life; it may be carefully over-compensated later on; as a rule one part of it is overcome while another part persists.[21]

Interestingly, in view of Stolorow and Atwood's analysis of Freud's own early development, the seeds of the little girl's hostility are seen as sown when the birth of a sibling arouses jealousy. Freud even writes, 'a child, even with an age difference of only eleven months, is not too young to take notice of what is happening'.[22] He was eleven months old when his brother Julius was born. Stolorow and Atwood conclude:

> We find in these contrasting accounts of psychosexual development for the boy and girl evidence of a defensive splitting of the maternal imago. In Freud's description of the boy's Oedipal development, the idealized image of his mother is preserved, harking back to the golden age before she betrayed him by disturbing their perfect union with unwanted intruders.

Notwithstanding a few scattered exceptions, the split-off image of the hated, faithless, depriving and disappointing mother is reserved primarily for his account of the girl's psychosexual development, where presumably it did not threaten to expose his own repressed rage at her. Further, as noted by Tomkins, the despised attributes of the repressed, split-off image of Freud's mother reappear in his conception of the inevitable outcome of female development. In Freud's view, because the girl feels herself to be already castrated, she lacks the most powerful motive enforcing superego formation, and her insufficient superego consolidation accounts for the emotional capriciousness and undeveloped sense of justice she will supposedly display as an adult.[23] In this notion of the woman's deficient superego, we see an encapsulation of Freud's unconscious grievance against the treacherous mother who, from his vantage point, capriciously dethroned him and unjustly prejudiced his rights to her exclusive love.

In short, we believe that in Freud's theory of psychosexual development not only is the source of badness transposed into the child in order to absolve the mother of blame but the good and bad aspects of the mother are also defensively kept separate in order to ward off his intense unconscious ambivalence conflict.[24]

You may not find this analysis totally convincing. As has been emphasized, any interpretation of this kind can only be a speculation. But it is useful in suggesting how a theory can be dependent on the characteristics of its originator and how its strengths and weaknesses may arise. It reminds us too of the caution necessary in applying the theory outside the context in which it was developed. While an Oedipus complex may have been of great importance to Freud and even his patients, it does not necessarily follow that it will apply to people from societies with different patterns of family life.

Being able to identify the personal and contextual origins of a theory should not be assumed to undermine its value. *Every* theory is a construction. None is immune from being influenced by the theorist. Psychobiographical analyses of this kind can alert us to obvious bias. They highlight the fact that personality theories are not objective statements of general laws and are limited in their scope. Each offers a somewhat different perspective for making sense of human beings. It is likely to overemphasize some aspects and neglect others. But people differ too. Human experience is inevitably individual and derived from a particular personal history. One theory may be effectively applied to this person but not to another. Thus different theories can usefully co-exist.

CHAPTER 13

Moral Implications and Social Impact

The relations between one person and another, between individual and social context, between a theorist and his theory are all two way. Each influences the other. As Erich Fromm has expressed the dialectical relationship between individual and society: 'Man is not only made by history – history is made by man . . . passions, desires, anxieties change and develop as a result of the social process, but also . . . man's energies thus shaped into specific forms in their turn become productive forces, moulding the social process'.[1] Freud's theory, as we have seen, was a product of a particular personal and social background. In its turn, it changed, not only Freud's life, but the conception of Man prevalent in Western society. Philip Rieff has pointed out that Freud 'is not only the first completely irreligious moralist, he is a moralist without even a moralising message'.[2] Freud, with the characteristic detachment of a scientist of his time, considered value judgements to have no place in his theory. Yet paradoxically his theories do have important ethical implications. Absorbed into our culture, they have demonstrated their potential to change the ways we behave and the moral judgements we make. The purpose of this chapter is to consider briefly this influence. What moral implications does psychoanalysis have? And what kind of impact has it had on the society in which we live?

During his later life, in a series of works which included *Totem and Taboo,*[3] *The Future of an Illusion*[4] and *Civilization and its Discontents,*[5] Freud turned his attention more specifically to trying to understand the origins and effects of society and its institutions. The first of these is a set of four essays in which he draws comparisons between neurotic processes and the pattern of social life found in primitive societies. He argues that the ritual practice of taboos and totemism (i.e., when an animal or object is venerated but may be sacrificed on special occasions) represents a collective defence against prohibited desires for incest and murder. Drawing on anthropological work, he speculates that the origins of the incest taboo and totemism lay in the killing, long ago, of the father–leader by the younger men of a primal horde. They arise from their need for expiation of guilt and for social control once the feared leader has been dethroned. In essence, Freud is arguing that the Oedipus complex is rooted in the history and conventions of society and not just in the individual family. His argument depends on some rather suspect anthropological material (the notion of the primal horde) and possibly the dubious implication that acquired behaviour and beliefs can somehow be inherited. He seemed inclined himself to regard the monograph only as speculation. He is reported, some years later, as having dismissed its central idea of primal parricide with the remark, 'Oh don't take that seriously – I made that up on a rainy Sunday afternoon'.[6]

In *Totem and Taboo*, Freud presents religion as a form of communal neurosis, its rituals serving as defences against prohibited desires. *The Future of an Illusion* develops this theme. In the third book, *Civilization and its Discontents*, Freud postulates that the relationship between the individual and society is of a fundamentally antithetical kind. Instinctual needs have to be repressed in order that people may live together. Aggression is controlled by introjection by the superego in the form of guilt. Freud sees guilt as the most important problem arising from the development of civilization. 'The price we pay for our civilization is a loss of happiness through the heightening of the sense of guilt'.[7] This again was a development of an idea which had made its appearance earlier. In *The Question of Lay Analysis*,[8] he had suggested the analytic training of a band of social workers as a corrective against the 'almost intolerable pressure' our society imposes.

These works on society represent speculative extensions of his more central ideas. For this reason and because they are not focused on personality dynamics, they were not covered in the earlier exposition of Freud's work. In any case, they are among the most controversial of his writings. Later analysts, particularly Kardiner, Fromm and Erikson, have made more sophisticated attempts to apply psychoanalytic concepts to the study of society. The intention in this section is not to review in detail these specific ideas of Freud about the nature and origins of society but rather to see what implications are carried by the central tenets of psychoanalysis themselves.

The reflexive nature of personality theories has already been referred to in the previous section. They carry the power to influence our conceptions of ourselves. As this in turn affects the way we are, it is important to consider what kind of model of the person psychoanalysis implies. Looking back over the previous sections, we can see that, like Freud's theory though in a somewhat different way, it has a double face. In one sense it is deterministic. Psychic determinism is a central prop of psychoanalytic theory. Nothing is seen as accidental. Even the smallest gesture, the most unnoticed act has its significance. And yet, at the same time, psychoanalysis is fundamentally concerned with our capacity to transcend the influences acting upon us. With the help of insight, we can gain control over our destiny. On one hand then it sees mankind as the pawn of forces of biology and environment, on the other as capable, because of the power of insight, of shaping what we are. This combination of determinism and autonomy may seem contradictory. And yet only perhaps because of the limitations of our thinking – our preferences for clear-cut categories of *either* . . . *or* rather than what may be a more realistic paradox. For, as suggested earlier, it could be argued that such an amalgam is appropriate for it reflects the double nature of humanity. On one hand we *are* determined by forces outside our control. On the other, we live as active participants (agents) in the world, capable of warding off its influences, of manipulating it for our needs, our own actions creating the way things will be. You may be reminded here of the double process which Piaget postulates as being at the heart of understanding – accommodation and assimilation. Our awareness develops by responding to the world. But it is capable of imposing its categories on the world in its turn – a dialectic dance.

Because of this dual nature, the influence of psychoanalysis on our conception of ourselves (and hence the way we lead our lives) can take very different forms. A major effect of the theory is to make us more aware of the limitations of our awareness. It legitimates the notion that the origins of our actions lie outside our conscious selves. One result of this may be to undermine our sense of personal responsibility. How can we be to blame when the real reasons for our behaviour were unknown to us? Another may be to encourage a narcissistic self-absorption. Analysands in particular may become engaged in an interminable and often impossible quest for the hidden reasons for what they do. To modify a bitter aphorism of Karl Kraus – one of the wildest of Freud's contemporary critics – psychoanalysis becomes the disease for which it purports to be the cure.

Psychic determinism also has its impact on our relations with others. We read new significance into words and actions. There are amusing tales of the wariness which the publication of Freud's book on humour induced in colleagues. It is reported that at a lecture they would watch for Freud's response before laughing at a joke lest their spontaneous reaction gave unwitting clues about negative aspects of their inner selves. Brill enlarges on this aspect of their interactions in an addition he made in his translation of Freud's *The Psychopathology of Everyday Life*.

> Those were the pioneer days of Freud [and his theories] among psychiatrists, and we observed and studied and noted whatever was done

or said about us with unfailing patience and untiring interest and zeal. (We made no scruples, for instance, of asking a man at table why he did not use his spoon in the proper way, or why he did such and such a thing in such and such a manner.) It was impossible for one to show any degree of hesitation or make some abrupt pause in speaking without being at once called to account. We had to keep ourselves well in hand, ever ready and alert, for there was no telling when and where there would be a new attack. We had to explain why we whistled or hummed some particular tune or why we made some slip in talking or some mistake in writing. But we were glad to do this if for no other reason than to learn to face the truth.[9]

The need to treat psychoanalysis as a causal science often tempted Freud and his colleagues to emphasize psychic determinism to excess. The negative effects of this were noted by Otto Rank, himself for many years a member of Freud's inner circle.

I believe analysis has become the worst enemy of the soul. It killed what it analyzed. I saw too much psychoanalysis with Freud and his disciples which became pontifical and dogmatic. That was why I was ostracized from the original group. I became interested in the artist. I became interested in literature, in the magic of language. I disliked medical language, which was sterile.[10]

Other consequences of an attitude of psychic determinism are more positive. It may well be that alertness to the unconscious springs of actions has the power to extend our capacity for empathy. It may restrain us from standing in critical judgement on the deeds of others and ourselves and encourages us rather to see people as if in a Greek tragedy – characters inexorably playing out the whims and wishes of a fate which is not of our making.

Psychoanalysis is part of a sequence of philosophical and scientific developments which have served to dethrone Man from his sense of being central in the universe. Copernicus and Galileo began it by their insistence that the world goes round the sun. Darwin extended it by emphasizing the continuity between humanity and other species. Freud intensified it by showing us that, consciously at least, we are not even at the centre of ourselves. Marx achieved this too – though in a different way – by emphasizing how much we are at the mercy of economic and social conditions. The effects of this decentring process are paradoxical in themselves. On one hand, it serves to increase our sense of insignificance. This has its value in alleviating the burden we may otherwise feel in being responsible for what we do. On the other hand, it is a mark of our power – a manifestation of our extraordinary capacity to understand our origins and what we are. For Freud and Marx at least, this became a powerful instrument for creating individual and social change. This other face of psychoanalysis conveys a message of a much more optimistic kind. While Freud encourages us to accept the reality of the power of our biological needs and of the past, he does not leave us as the total pawns of fate. Psychoanalysis is premised also on the power of reason and reflection. By struggling for insight, we are capable of bringing the unruly elements of our unconscious into awareness and under our autonomous control. With the help of introspection and working through, we may hope that 'where id was' we may 'let ego be'. Although psychoanalytic theory is rooted then in a determinist view of human life, its very existence is a powerful support in the human struggle for autonomy. This struggle expresses itself in different forms. The growth of technology has marked the increasing control by the human species over the environment on which it depends. Revolution and political reform testify at least our capacity to change the social conditions under which we live. The contribution of psychoanalysis is towards increased awareness of ourselves and therefore, we may hope, to greater mastery of the ways in which we act and feel.

So far, this discussion has centred on the *implications* of Freud's model of the person for our moral and social life. According to Erikson,[11] once when Freud was asked what people should be able to do well, he did venture a direct prescription for healthy living. His advice was '*Lieben und arbeiten*' (to love and to work). Generally, though, Freud was wary of such pronouncements. In the opening sentence of *Civilization and its Discontents* he asserts; 'It is impossible to escape the impression that people commonly use false standards of measurement – that they seek power, success and wealth for themselves and admire them in others, and that they underestimate what is of true value in life'.[12] He was not though inclined to give specific advice on what true value should be. The essence of the psychoanalytic position is the acceptance of reality in so far as we can determine this. The aim of analysis is to get the patient to live his life without the prop of beliefs which lack conscious rational bases. Such an approach inevitably leads to a debunking of accepted values and ethical principles by attributing to these a meaning very different from that which they presume. In Freud's terms, perversion is no longer a sin, it is literally childishness; religious belief as a denial of the painful realities of death and insignificance, partakes of the quality of neurosis; at least some (though, of course, by no means all) revolutionary fervour becomes individual expression of a replay of childish revolt against the father, and unthinking patriotism a mere re-enactment of childhood submission. Whether or not the specific Freudian explanations are precisely the correct ones is not the point. The fact that such clearly held convictions *may* have their origins in the chance vagaries of development tends to undermine their potency.

But while psychoanalysis attempts to break down the illusions forced upon us by society and our own development, it fails to replace what it takes away. Thus, it can all too easily engender a form of nihilism. The effect of psychoanalysis on Western society has not necessarily been what Freud would have approved. Its undermining of dogmatic, moralistic systems and the exposition of the idea of the universality of instinctual demands must surely have provided an important impetus to launching a more permissive society – a less authoritarian educational system and a greater tolerance for sexual needs. Together, these may well have weakened what Weber has called the Protestant Ethic. To undermine beliefs, to reduce the need for sublimation, to lessen the guilt generated by early conflict may be, if one accepts a Freudian viewpoint, to adulterate the initiative, drive and purpose that led to the prosperity of industrialized Western society. You may welcome this or not (though it is worth bearing in mind that the economic effects of such a development may not be so important in a society where greater automation and organizational effectiveness is coupled with increasing unemployment and leisure time). To create an existential vacuum, as psychoanalysis has helped to do, is probably a necessary stage in the development of a saner society, but it can only be a beginning not an end.

CONCLUSION

CHAPTER 14

Explorations in Awareness

Looking back over this account and appraisal of psychoanalysis, one of the major issues to emerge is what *kind* of knowledge of ourselves we can expect to have. The clear message of the book has been that all understanding is a construction of some kind, dependent on whatever assumptions, characteristics, contexts and values define the perspective of the understander in question. The paradox of research is that we need to know something of what it is we are looking for before we can hope to find out what it is. We cannot start without assumptions and a perspective but we need to be prepared to discard them, like a no-longer-needed crutch, once our research is under way. Hence the importance of metaperspective – being able to step back from the enterprise of investigation and reflect on its nature and the assumptions which underlie it.

We live in an age of machines. This encourages us to demand definitiveness and precision. Many academic attempts to understand the self have started from the implicit assumption that psychological life is somehow like a material commodity. There is a temptation to assume that it has some kind of definitive essence which it is possible, though by no means easy, for us to precisely ascertain and investigate. The approach of academic psychology has characteristically been reductionist – to attempt to reduce the phenomena of self and psychological life to simple and more manageable forms which can be specified in terms of observable operations and measures. Research has tended to rest too on the presumption of linear causality, that any observed event can be attributed to an underlying cause of a potentially identifiable kind; and on the aspiration that, with the help of the method of experiment, it is possible to identify such causes and build up a set of laws to account for human behaviour in a general way. In the past, psychologists have often adopted a nineteenth century concept of scientific method. Today, most have a more sophisticated view. In keeping with twentieth-century physics they acknowledge, if only implicitly, the constructed and relative nature of the knowledge they pursue. But even now the reductionist and nomothetic approach, the assumption of linear causality rules the day – not surprisingly perhaps in a machine age where the power of this approach has so increased our understanding of the physical world; and given the seductive attraction of the view that self and mental life can be dealt with in a similar way.

This was the premise from which Freud began. But instead of forcing the recalcitrant phenomena of mental life into an inappropriate mould, Freud hovered, never, as has been argued, fully resolving the conflict between his desire for a scientific method and the appreciation of its inability to capture the subject-matter he sought to understand. It was perhaps only because neo-Freudians such as Erikson had not been socialized like Freud in the methods of natural science that they were more easily able to acknowledge that 'man, the subject of psychosocial science, will not hold still enough to be divided into categories both measurable and relevant'.[1]

But why not? What is it about the self that renders it unamenable to an investigative procedure which has proved its worth so well elsewhere? In this book I have tried to offer some answer to this question.

In part, it might be thought attributable to the complexity of the different aspects of self and the interrelationships between them. But complexity itself has not stood in the way of applying scientific method. It has provided all the more reason for it. The key issue concerns the nature of the aspects to be interrelated. As we have seen, these are of very different kinds and have traditionally been the province of different disciplines. The self is rooted in biological process – in the needs, vulnerabilities, potentials and limitations of the person as a biological organism. It is intrinsically interwoven too with symbolic process, in the meanings attributed consciously or unconsciously to the world around, assimilated from the social contexts through language and direct contact with other people, or learned through actual experience. So the self is at once biological and social, dependent on both physiological and symbolic process, on the physical and experiential. Although there is clearly an intimate interdependence between these two realms, I have asserted that there is a fundamental distinction between them in that one is not reducible to the other. This is a primary source of the difficulty of studying their integration – the need to find a common language or concept system to span them both and explore their interface. This integrative function, it has been argued, is what psychoanalysis makes a brave attempt to fulfil.

In psychological life meaning is paramount. Much of the impact of the physical realm on our lives is mediated through its offices. Many biological characteristics assume significance largely or entirely because of the meaning attributed to them by others. Even death may be experienced as triumph or despair depending on the meaning with which it is imbued.

The problem confronted by any student of psychological life is the elusive nature of meaning as subject-matter. Not only is its representation and understanding a construction but it is itself a construction with all the variability and perspective-dependence that implies. Meaning is constantly in flux, constantly being negotiated and renegotiated through our conversations and actions and reflecting on what we do. As we reach out to grasp it, so we change it in so doing. As the self is constituted by meanings so these characteristics apply to it as well. For example, when we communicate to someone our explanation of why they are as they are, that in itself is likely to change the person that it purports to account for. This is not just, like the Heisenberg principle, an essentially methodological issue, but one which has implications for the very nature of the self.

In studying the self we need to change the assumptions on which such research has so often been based, to move towards a more specifically *psychosocial* science. Such a science would reflect the three primary themes which emerge from this book. First, its methods and expectations should be geared to the centrality and significance of meanings in mental and social life. They will thus be directed at the hermeneutic task of eliciting and representing configurations of meaning. Second, its concepts and approach will attempt to encompass and interrelate the complex roots of self in biology, social process and individual development. Third, it will be reflexive, continually alert to the origins of its own constructions and the impact of the acts of investigation and explanation upon the subjects it seeks to understand.

As we have seen in this book, psychoanalysis has made a useful beginning in all these respects. In effect it contains within itself the makings of a *dialectical psychology*. Dialectic is a term used in different contexts to carry a variety of connotations. Here I use it to indicate three broad principles on which a truly psychosocial science would be grounded, and conversely, to indicate the kind of understanding about self which it would be futile to expect.

First of all, if we assume that our subject-matter is in constant flux, that it is always changing, then we need to look at *process* – the ways in which change comes about, and not search for essences. In contrast to an absolutist search for general laws and statements about the way people are, psychoanalysis generally conceptualizes the self in terms of the processes of change and development on which it depends.

Second, we have a situation where each aspect of self influences every other aspect. So the effects of physical disability or an abnormally high level of physiological drive will very much depend on the social context in which it occurs and the meanings therefore attributed to it. Each aspect can only be properly conceptualized and understood by seeing it in relation to the others. Contrast this with the positivist notion of characteristics which can be isolated and objectively assessed. We might also query how far, given such dependence on interrelationships, experiments designed to yield general laws about unidirectional causes are appropriate either.

Static and linear forms of explanation have little or no place, for our third principle asserts that meanings emerge from the interplay of different and often contradictory forces. This, as we have seen, has been a basic premise on the psychoanalytic position with its concern to explore the kinds of psychic interplay which can occur and their effects. Analysts like Jung and Erikson have gone even further than Freud in emphasizing that the dynamic interaction of polarities or oppositional tendencies is a fundamental feature cf psychological and social life. Contrast this with an approach which conceptualizes personality as a set of positions on a profile of dimensions. Such a theory conceives of a person as *either* introvert or extravert, loving *or* hating, or at some point in between. But in dialectical psychology, the poles are thought of as dynamic tensions rather than cancelling each other out. From their interplay actions and experiences emerge. So from the co-existence of love and hate may come a passionate ambivalence rather than a state of lukewarm indifference.

The aim of such a dialectical psychology is not to produce a definitive and unchanging account of the self, and a set of general laws explaining how and why each aspect has come about. Rather, it is to provide the means for *explorations in awareness*; for alerting us to the complex of meanings which generate and inform our actions and experiences. It should strive for rigour nonetheless. There are still criteria to be applied as a measure of the adequacy of the accounts of meaning it yields.[2] One is *differentiation* – the degree to which it provides a detailed pattern encompassing the salient aspects of the behaviours or situations we are trying to understand. Another is *consistency*. How well do all the various aspects of meaning we can elicit fit together in a coherent whole? Such criteria are not easy to apply. Nor is it always possible in the case of consistency to be precise about the fit. Ideally, consistency might be tested against predictions generated on the basis of the meaning patterns assumed. In practice, this is more easily said than done; particularly because, as we have noted, meaning patterns tend to be in constant flux and may change their character radically in a short space of time. Nevertheless in spite of such difficulties, differentiation and consistency are quite probably the best criteria we can aspire to.

The value of psychoanalysis is in the tools and concepts it provides for helping us to explore and become more aware of the self and its potentials in everyday living. This is a process which can be greatly helped by other people whom you can trust and get close to – intimate friends, fellow-members of a growth or encounter group or therapist. By working through experiences with them and by mutual sharing, comment and reflection, you may come to an awareness of aspects of yourself and their integration greater than that which you can achieve on your own. But although with self-reflection you can get locked into circles from which it is difficult to break out and see the way forward, much can be achieved in this way as well. Try taking the concepts and ideas which have been presented in this book and applying them to your self and your own life situation. For example, try to identify any inner conflicts and tensions within yourself. From what do they stem? Are there any particularly characteristic defence mechanisms you use to protect yourself from anxiety or cope with trauma? Do you typically repress painful experiences, deny or project them or use reaction formation or isolation etc.? Although these defences are usually unconscious, careful observation of yourself may give you some clues as to whether you use them. These are difficult issues and permit of no easy hard-and-fast answers. But the concepts and the discussion of them in the text may help you to explore your self a little more deeply or at least alert your attention to possible aspects and ways of thinking about them. For those of you interested in pursuing this, I have included in an appendix a few gentle exercises which may help to facilitate the process.

In all this, of course, it is important to bear in mind the theme of this chapter. Understanding of mental life is process not essence. In other words, it will consist of ongoing, dynamic, changing patterns of awareness. There will never be a definitive hard-and-fast account of the way you are and why (or at least not one that is valid). A paradox of the nature of human understanding is that the more we develop our power to understand, the more we realize the limitations of what we can ever know. But we might hope at least for a little more differentiation in awareness, an opening up to possibilities, that the pieces we are aware of begin to cohere and make a little more sense. Psychoanalysis at its best can help us to see a little more clearly and free us a little from the burdens of our past, alerting us the influence of infantile anxieties on our lives both as individuals and nations, helping us to realize that:

> Every adult, whether he is a follower or a leader, a member of a mass or of an *élite*, was once a child. He was once small. A sense of smallness forms a substratum in his mind, ineradicably. His triumphs will be measured against this smallness, his defeats will substantiate it. The questions as to who is bigger and who can do or not do this or that, and to whom – these questions fill the adult's inner life far beyond the necessities and the desirabilities which he understands and for which he plans.[3]

But our lives are not merely an expression of our pasts. Potentially at least they are moral and creative acts. If this is only implicit in Freud's writings, some later analysts like Erikson are prepared to acknowledge it more openly. In his characteristically visual style, Erikson conceptualizes the achievements of psychoanalysis in terms of movement in different dimensions.

> It had turned *inward* to open up man's inner world, and especially the unconscious, to systematic study; it searched *backward* to the ontogenetic origins of the mind and of its disturbances; and it pressed *downward* into those instinctual tendencies which man thought he had overcome when he repressed or denied the infancy of individuals, the primitivity of man's beginnings – and evolution . . .

He points out though that it needs also to lead:

> *Outward* from self-centredness to the mutuality of love and communality, *forward* from the enslaving past to the utopian anticipation of new potentialities, and *upward* from the unconscious to the enigma of consciousness.[4]

Erikson is pointing here, I think, to our need not just to understand our past but to create new directions: not just to come to terms with what we are but to create what will be.

Each of us is steered through the landscape of life by forces over which we ultimately have no control. We did not choose the time and place of our birth, nor who our parents were to be, our genetic inheritance or how we were to be reared. We did not determine the culture in which we emerged and the attitudes, values, beliefs and role models which we have assimilated and which have assimilated us. We are set on course and constrained by the combinations these represent. Our future too will be in large part decided by terrain not of our making. How much say will we have in the shaping of the society in which we will live out our days, even where and how we will die?

But yet again there is paradox. Even given the web of 'outside' control, the remarkable fact is that most of us every day experience a breathtaking scope of potential for self-direction and self-control. We assume this daily. As groups, societies and individuals, we struggle to create our future, planning activities, devising schedules, deciding when and how things shall be. We may find that others conspire to frustrate us or deprive us of the resources we need; that unknown forces within us cloud our emotions or undermine that which we seek to feel or to be. But it is through glimpsed insights of the kind which psychoanalysis can offer, opening ourselves up to possibilities, coming to terms with the need to both accept and create what we are, and working with the contradictions of existence rather than striving to deny them, that each of us can learn to take up with a little more courage and imagination our own role in understanding and creating ourselves.

APPENDIX

Exercises in Self-Awareness

Opening Up Awareness

Our heads are full of thoughts, anxieties, wishes, concern about the past and future. It is not always easy to focus our awareness on what we are experiencing, to introspect upon our feelings. These first two exercises are intended to help you to do this.

1 *Getting inside yourself*

Find a quiet place where you will not be disturbed and lie on the floor with your eyes closed. Breathe slowly and deeply but easily and try to relax your body as far as you can. Then, focus on your right foot and leg. Tense them hard. Hold this tension for three to four seconds, then relax. Repeat this tensing and relaxing procedure twice. Continue in the same fashion, tensing and relaxing three times in succession the left leg and foot, buttocks and pelvis, pressing the pit of the back to the floor, tensing and relaxing chest and shoulders, right arm and hand, left arm and hand, shoulders and face muscles. Lie still again, breathing slowly and deeply but in a relaxed way. Try consciously to ease any tensions. Once or twice, tense up your whole body, hold it tense for several seconds, then relax back again as before. Try to empty your mind.

Focus your attention on the soles of your feet. Imagine yourself entering your body at that point and slowly wander up the legs and explore each part of the body. Try to become aware of every sensation in the part on which you are focusing – pressures, tensions, aches, pains, feelings, cold, warmth, expansions, etc. Focus on sensation: don't try to evaluate or think what you should feel. Experience. Keeping your eyes shut, become aware of the different parts of your body and their relationship to each other. (If you feel like moving or stretching at any point, feel free to do so.)

This exercise should be repeated over several days. Gradually you should become aware of sensations within you that you normally ignore.

2   *Here and now*

The aim of this activity is to encourage you to focus as intensively as possible on your immediate flow of awareness – on what you experience *here and now*.

1. Make yourself comfortable and relax for a while, breathing slowly, steadily and deeply, but without effort.
2. Let your mind focus on whatever you can see, hear, smell and taste. You might like to focus on each modality in turn, or you may prefer to allow whichever sense dominates your attention at any one time to do so. Try to be aware both of what you are experiencing (e.g., I am aware of a silky patterned blue surface; I am aware of a noise like a car engine revving up in the distance) and also of what the process of being consciously aware of focusing your attention in this way feels like (e.g., does it give you a sense of alertness or aliveness?).
3. After a while, close your eyes and shift your attention to bodily sensations and feelings. Are you aware, for example, of the sensation of your clothes against your skin and, if you are sitting, the pressure of the seat against your backside? Can you sense any tension? Where? Or does your body feel completely relaxed?
4. Turn your focus on your feelings. What are you feeling at this particular moment? If that feeling leads to a chain of further emotions or even thoughts, let them come, all the time trying to experience fully each emotion as it arises. Some people claim that if you can give yourself up fully to any negative feeling which arises – such as jealousy, guilt or resentment – then it disappears. Giving yourself up to positive feelings, however, intensifies them. Try this out when you can and see if it works for you.
5. Finally, let your mind go free, following whatever fantasy or image emerges.

If you can, also try this exercise with a partner. In this case, express your experience aloud. Your partner's task is to help keep you focused on your 'here and now' experience and to stop you thinking about events or thoughts outside this, or thinking *about* your experience rather than directly experiencing. When your mind starts to wander, he or she should try to bring you back to focusing on what you are aware of.

In everyday living, try to become more aware of impulses within yourself – the way you feel, what you want. Admit them to full awareness (you do not necessarily have to act on them!) Try to focus on what you really feel not on the way you think you are supposed to feel. Open yourself too to 'peak experiences' – those occasional moments of experience when an image, feeling, sight or sound fills you with delight. When and if such moments occur, stop for a while and focus your total awareness on them.

Exploring the Unconscious

3   *Recording dreams*

Try making a record of your dreams. There is evidence that almost all of us dream every night though we may not remember having done so when we awake. To facilitate recall of your dreams, keep a pen and paper by your bed so that you can write out your dreams in as much detail as possible as soon as you awake, before you have forgotten them or they are too distorted in your memory. Note any events of the previous day to which the dream content seems to relate. If you can not remember dreaming, lie quietly and see what images or ideas arise in your mind. Free associating to these may well lead you to remember your dream. You may find it helpful also to tell yourself several times before dropping off to sleep that you will remember your dreams the following morning.

When you have a series of dreams or dream fragments on record, look through them to see if there are any patterns, images or emotions which seem to emerge. You might like to try free associating to any key symbols or images that continually occur. Do not expect your own analysis of dream content to yield necessarily fundamental information about yourself, but it may provide useful insights and a stimulus to self reflection.

4   *Defence mechanisms*

Make a list of the defence mechanisms discussed in Chapter 5. Are there any which you think you characteristically tend to use to cope with anxiety or difficult situations. Try to identify two or three particularly problematic or traumatic times in your life. Think them through and jot down notes on what happened in each case. How did you react? Can you detect any typical patterns of defence in your behaviours and ways of thinking about them? Would there have been a more effective way to have coped?

5   *Psychosexual styles*

Look back over Freud's stages of psychosexual development discussed in Chapter 4 and their associated personality styles. Think about these in relation to your self. Are there any oral or anal type gratifications which give you particular pleasure for example? Can you detect any of the characteristics described in your own personality?

6 *Images of self*

As we have seen in the discussion of Freud's theory of the unconscious, much of our most potent and emotional awareness comes in the form of images and sensations rather than words. Trying to think of yourself and your identity through images, as opposed to articulating this in words, may throw up some interesting insights.

Note down the metaphors which you feel best describe what you feel yourself to be (e.g., a reefed ship sailing through rough seas, a bud about to burst into flower, a house falling apart at the seams etc.). Go through these and analyse their properties. Why do they seem to fit you and your situation?

Another more unusual and difficult technique which some people find produces interesting results, is to imagine entering your self and travelling deep into its inner layers. Open yourself to whatever images spontaneously arise. This is best done while relaxed in a quiet and darkened room. You may find yourself encountering scenes from your past or childhood, or images of places and events which somehow seem to personify you. Do not hurry or force the journey. Let the images arise as far as possible of their own accord. Do not analyse them, just experience them. Afterwards, you can recall and examine them for what they might tell you about your self and feelings.

7 *Transference*

1. Think of several specific people whom you love and/or admire. Jot down brief notes of the kinds of people they are. How would you describe them? What is it about them that you particularly like? Is there anything about them that you find irritating?
2. Do the same with your parents. What kind of people are/were they? Try to do this in terms of how you see them now and how you did when you were growing up.
3. Look back over your notes. Are there patterns and consistencies? Do they tell you anything about your own self and the ideals you aspire to?

Try to be alert as far as you can, to the influence of transference, both positive and negative, in your current relationships. How are they coloured by the emotional feelings you felt towards your family and others in early life?

Freeing yourself from the past

8 *Creating an action*

1. Think of something you would like to do but would not ordinarily do (e.g., going to a museum, taking a taxi instead of a bus, giving a present to someone, speaking to someone you would like to get to know).
2. Imagine yourself doing this.
3. Do it. Be aware that you have chosen to do it and have created an action which otherwise would not have happened.

9 *Creating your life*

Gradually widen the scope of this exercise. Try behaving towards others, for example, in a way that you would like to but would not normally do. Try setting events in train which you would like to happen but would not normally bother, hope or dare to bring about.

You should begin by setting aside an undisturbed period of time for these activities. But gradually try, as with the concepts and ideas presented in the book, to incorporate them into the pattern of your everyday life, becoming more aware of the significances and possibilities of the self you seem to be and the self you can become.

References and Notes

Standard Edition refers to J. Strachey (editor 1953–66) *The Complete Psychological Works of Sigmund Freud, vols. I–XXIV*, London, Hogarth Press

Chapter 1 – The Individual as Integrator

1. E. H. Erikson (1968) *Identity: Youth and Crisis*, London, Faber.
2. L. Rhinehart (1972) *The Diceman*, London, Panther.
3. See, for example, R. B. Cattell (1965) *The Scientific Analysis of Personality*, Harmondsworth, Penguin; H. J. Eysenck (1947) *Dimensions of Personality*, London, Routledge and (1952) *The Scientific Study of Personality*, London, Routledge.
4. For more detailed discussion of this issue see J. Israel (1975) 'Stipulations and construction in the social sciences' in H. Brown and R. Stevens (eds.) *Social Behaviour and Experience: Multiple Perspectives*, London, Hodder and Stoughton; and R. Stevens (1976) *Understanding Social Behaviour and Experience*, Social Psychology, Block 1, Milton Keynes, The Open University Press.
5. See, for example, R. D. Stolorow and G. E. Atwood (1979) *Faces in a Cloud: Subjectivity in Personality Theory*, New York, Aronson.
6. See, for example, A. C. Elms (1981) 'Skinner's dark year and *Walden Two*', *American Psychologist*, 36, (5), pp. 470–9.
7. J. Israel (1975) *op. cit.*

Chapter 2 – Freud – the Man

1. See S. Freud (1961) *Letters of Sigmund Freud*, selected and edited by E. L. Freud, London, Hogarth Press.
2. S. Freud (1930) *Civilization and its Discontents*, Standard Edition, vol. XXI.
3. E. Jones (1953-7) *The Life and Work of Sigmund Freud*, London, Hogarth Press. Abridged by L. Trilling and S. Marcus (1964), Harmondsworth, Penguin.
4. See O. Gillie and P. Swales (1982) 'The secret love life of Sigmund Freud', *The Sunday Times*, 1 January 1982. But in 'Freud and Minna', *Psychology Today* (December 1982) Alan Elms provides a thoughtful critique of Swales' assertions and concludes that they have little foundation.
5. S. Freud (1910) *Leonardo da Vinci and a Memory of his Childhood*, Standard Edition, vol. XI.
6. S. Freud (1963) *Psychoanalysis and Faith: the Letters of Sigmund Freud and Oskar Pfister*, edited by E. L. Freud and H. Meng, London, Hogarth Press.
7. S. Freud (1926) *The Question of Lay Analysis*, Standard Edition, vol. XX, p. 246.

Chapter 3 – The Unconscious

1. J. Breuer and S. Freud (1895) *Studies in Hysteria*, Standard Edition, vol. II, pp. 34–5.
2. S. Freud (1923) *The Ego and the Id*, Standard Edition, vol. XIX.
3. R. Dalbiez (1941) *Psychoanalytical Method and the Doctrine of Freud*, trans. by J. F. Lindsay, London, Longmans Green, p. 54.
4. R. I. Munroe (1955) *Schools of Psychoanalytic Thought*, New York, Holt, Rinehart and Winston, pp. 39–40.
5. *ibid.*, p. 40.
6. S. Freud (1900) *The Interpretation of Dreams*, Standard Edition, vol. IV, p. 175.
7. Cited by Munroe (1955) *op. cit.*
8. S. Freud (1950) *The Interpretation of Dreams*, trans. by A. A. Brill, New York, Random House, pp. 189–90.
9. S. Freud (1900) *op. cit.*, p. 196.
10. S. Freud (1950) *op. cit.*, p. 335.
11. S. Freud (1950) *op. cit.*, p. 242.
12. S. Freud (1901) *The Psychopathology of Everyday Life*, Standard Edition, vol. VI.
13. S. Freud (1910) *The Psychopathology of Everyday Life*, (3rd edition) trans. by A. A. Brill (1914) London, Ernest Benn, pp. 63–4.
14. *ibid.*, pp. 136–7.
15. B. Bettelheim (1982) 'Reflections. Freud and the soul', *The New Yorker*, March 1st.

Chapter 4 – Psychosexual Development

1. See, for example, J. Bowlby (1952) *Maternal Care and Mental Health*, WHO monograph, 2nd edition; (1979) *Making and Breaking of Affectional Bonds*, London, Tavistock; H. G. Harlow (1958) 'The nature of love', *American Psychologist*, vol. 13, pp. 673–85.
2. J. Bowlby (1971) *Attachment*, Harmondsworth, Penguin.
3. S. Freud (1920) *Beyond the Pleasure Principle*, Standard Edition, vol. XVIII.
4. *ibid.*, p. 38.
5. S. Freud (1905) *Three Essays on Sexuality*, Standard Edition, vol. VII, p. 186.
6. *ibid.*
7. S. Freud (1908) 'Character and anal erotism', Standard Edition, vol. IX, p. 169.
8. S. Freud (1925) 'Some psychical consequences of the anatomical distinction between the sexes', Standard Edition, vol. XIX; (1931) *Female Sexuality*, Standard Edition, vol. XXI.
9. If you are interested in pursuing the controversy further, see Juliet Mitchell's (1974) account and critique in *Psychoanalysis and Feminism*, London, Allen Lane.
10. S. Freud (1905) *op. cit.*, p. 165.

Chapter 5 – Psychodynamics

1. S. Freud (1923) *The Ego and the Id,* Standard Edition, vol. XIX.
2. B. Bettelheim (1982) 'Reflections. Freud and the Soul', *The New Yorker,* March 1st, p. 83.
3. *Ibid.,* p. 80.
4. See especially *The Ego and the Id* (1923) *op. cit.,* and *Inhibitions, Symptoms and Anxiety* (1926), Standard Edition, vol. XX.
5. Anna Freud (1936) *The Ego and Mechanisms of Defence,* trans. by C. Baines (1966), London, Hogarth Press.
6. T. W. Adorno, E. Frenkel-Brunswik, D. J. Levinson and R. Nevitt Sanford. (1950) *The Authoritarian Personality,* New York, Harper and Row.
7. R. I. Munroe (1955) *Schools of Psychoanalytic Thought,* New York, Holt, Rinehart and Winston.
8. S. Freud (1909) *Analysis of a Phobia in a Five-Year Old Boy,* Standard Edition, vol. X.
9. See, for example, Erik Erikson (1950) *Childhood and Society,* New York, Norton (Reprinted in paperback (1977) by Triad/Paladin.)
10. B. Bettelheim (1943) 'Individual and mass behaviour in extreme situations', *Journal of Abnormal and Social Psychology,* 38, pp. 417–52.
11. *The Sunday Times* (1974) 'Hidden persuaders in hostage war', *Insight* report, 3 November.

Chapter 6 – Theory of Neurosis

1. S. Freud (1917) *Introductory Lectures on Psychoanalysis,* Standard Edition, vol. XVI, p. 426.
2. S. Freud (1940) *An Outline of Psychoanalysis,* Standard Edition, vol. XXIII. p. 183.
3. S. Freud (1917) *op. cit.*
4. S. Freud (1909) *Notes Upon a Case of Obsessional Neurosis,* Standard Edition, vol. X, p. 158.
5. S. Freud (1940) *op. cit.,* p. 186.
6. S. Freud (1899) in *The Origins of Psychoanalysis: Letters to Wilhelm Fliess, Drafts and Notes, (1887–1902),* edited by M. Bonaparte, A. Freud and E. Kris (1954) London, Imago, p. 127.
7. O. Rank (1929) *The Trauma of Birth,* London, Kegan Paul. (Reissued (1973) New York, Harper and Row.)
8. See C. H. Thigpen and H. M. Cleckley (1974) *The Three Faces of Eve,* New York, Popular Library.

Chapter 7 – The Practice of Analysis as Therapy

1. S. Freud (1926) *The Question of Lay Analysis,* Standard Edition, vol. XX, p. 205.
2. G. H. Pollock (1976) 'Josef Breuer'. In J. E. Gedo and G. H. Pollock (eds.) *The Fusion of Science and Humanism. The Intellectual History of Psychoanalysis. Psychological Issues,* Monograph 34–5.

Chapter 8 – Freud's Progeny – Developments in Psychoanalysis

1. S. Freud (1920) *Beyond the Pleasure Principle*, Standard Edition, vol. XVIII.
2. See, for example, E. Jones (1964) *The Life and Work of Sigmund Freud*, abridged by L. Trilling and S. Marcus, Harmondsworth, Penguin.
3. S. Freud (1930) *Civilization and its Discontents*, Standard Edition, vol. XXI.
4. P. Roazen (1976) *Freud and his Followers*, London, Allen Lane.
5. H. Hartmann (1964) *Essays in Ego Psychology*, New York, International Universities Press.
6. E. Fromm (1974) *The Anatomy of Human Destructiveness*, London, Cape, p. 225.
7. *ibid*.
8. E. Fromm (1957) *The Art of Loving*, London, Unwin, pp. 16–17.
9. *ibid.*, p. 21.
10. E. Fromm (1964) *The Heart of Man: its Genius for Good and Evil*, New York, Harper and Row.
11. E. Fromm (1976) *To Have or To Be?* New York, Harper and Row.
12. E. Fromm (1947) *Man for Himself*, London, Routledge and Kegan Paul, p. 45.
13. K. Horney (1962) *Self-Analysis*, London, Routledge and Kegan Paul, p. 69.
14. *ibid.*, pp. 62–3.
15. K. Horney (1945) *Our Inner Conflicts*, New York, Norton, p. 117.
16. K. Horney (1962) *op. cit.*
17. In addition to the books cited above, see also K. Horney (1937) *Neurotic Personality of our Time*, (1939) *New Ways in Psychoanalysis*, (1950) *Neurosis and Human Growth*, New York, Norton.
18. E. Erikson (1950) *Childhood and Society*, New York, Norton. Reprinted in paperback (1977) by Triad/Paladin, p. 41.
19. E. H. Erikson (1959) *Young Man Luther: A study in psychoanalysis and history*, London, Faber.
20. E. H. Erikson (1969) *Gandhi's Truth*, London, Faber.
21. E. H. Erikson (1950) *op. cit.*, p. 256.
22. E. H. Erikson (1968) *Identity: Youth and Crisis*, London, Faber, p. 154.
23. E. H. Erikson (1950) *op. cit.*, p. 199.
24. For a more detailed account of see Erikson's work R. Stevens (1983) *Erik Erikson: an introduction*, Milton Keynes, The Open University Press.
25. H. Kohut (1977) *The Restoration of the Self*, New York, International Universities Press.
26. For example, see H. Doolittle (1956) *Tribute to Freud*, New York, McGraw-Hill.
27. See, for example, C. Brenner (1976) *Psychoanalytic Technique and Psychic Conflict*, New York, International Universities Press.
28. C. Brenner (1979) 'Working alliance, therapeutic alliance, and transference', *Journal of American Psychoanalytic Association*, Supplement, vol. 27, pp. 137–57.
29. For example, L. Stone (1961) *The Psychoanalytic Situation*, New York, International Universities Press.

30. R. R. Greenson (1967) *The Technique and Practice of Psychoanalysis*, New York, International Universities Press.
31. See, for example, J. Lacan (1977) *Ecrits: A Selection*, trans. by A. Sheridan, London, Tavistock.
32. J. Lacan (1968) *The Function of Language in Psychoanalysis*, Baltimore and London, The Johns Hopkins University Press, p. 9.
33. A. Lemaire (1977) *Jacques Lacan*, trans. by D. Macey, London, Routledge and Kegan Paul.
34. A. Wilden (1968) *The Language of the Self*, London, The Johns Hopkins University Press.
35. J. Boutonier (1950) in a review of the re-publication of Lacan's *Propos sur la Causalité Psychique*, 1947.
36. R. D. Laing (1977) *The Facts of Life*, Harmondsworth, Penguin.

Chapter 9 – Integration and Interpretation

1. S. Freud (1926) *The Question of Lay Analysis*, Standard Edition, vol. XX, pp. 126–7.
2. J. Grimm and W. Grimm (1968) *Fairy Tales*, London, Hamlyn.
3. B. Bettelheim (1976) *The Uses of Enchantment: The Meaning and Importance of Fairy Tales*, London, Thames and Hudson.

Chapter 10 – Psychoanalysis as Science

1. E. Fromm in R. I. Evans (1966) *Dialogue with Erich Fromm*, New York, Harper and Row.
2. B. F. Farrell (1981) *The Standing of Psychoanalysis*, Oxford, Oxford University Press.
3. L. L. Whyte (1978) *The Unconscious Before Freud*, London, Friedman.
4. *ibid.*, pp. 168–70.
5. H. Maudsley (1872) 'An address on medical psychology', *British Medical Journal*, 10, pp. 163–7.
6. R. von Krafft-Ebing (1899) *Psychopathia Sexualis*, London, Rebman.
7. A. Moll (1897) *Untersuchungen über die Libido sexualis*, Fischer's Medicinische Buchhandlung, Berlin, Kornfeld.
8. H. Ellis (1900) 'The analysis of the sexual impulse', *The Alienist and Neurologist*, 21, pp. 247–62.
9. See F. J. Sulloway (1979) *Freud, Biologist of the Mind*, London, Burnett Books, for an excellent review of the precursors of Freud's psychosexual theory.
10. S. Freud (1926) *The Question of Lay Analysis*, Standard Edition, vol. XX.
11. *ibid.*, p. 214.
12. S. Freud (1909) *Analysis of a Phobia in a Five-Year Old boy*, Standard Edition, vol. X.
13. L. Wittgenstein (1946) 'Conversations on Freud', in F. Cioffi (ed.) (1973) *Freud: Modern Judgements*, London, Macmillan.
14. B. A. Farrell (1981) *op. cit.*

15. For an excellent account of what it is like to undergo training as an analyst see J. Malcolm (1982) *Psychoanalysis: The Impossible Profession*, London, Picador.

16. S. Fisher and R. P. Greenberg (1977) *The Scientific Credibility of Freud's Theories and Therapy*, Hassocks, Harvester Press.

17. P. Kline (1972) *Fact and Fantasy in Freudian Theory*, London, Methuen; (1981) *Fact and Fantasy in Freudian Theory*, 2nd edition, London, Methuen.

18. R. M. Jones (1970) *The New Psychology of Dreaming*, New York, Grune and Stratton.

19. R. D. Cartwright, N. Bernick, G. Borowitz and A. Kling (1969) 'Effect of an erotic movie on the sleep and dreams of young men', *Archives of General Psychiatry*, 20, pp. 262–71.

20. H. A. Witkin (1969) 'Influencing dream content', in M. Kramer (ed.) *Dream Psychology and the New Biology of Dreaming*, Springfield, Thomas.

21. L. Breger, I. Hunter and R. W. Lane (1971) 'The effect of stress on dreams', *Psychological Issues*, 7, Monograph 27.

22. V. Castaldo and P. S. Holzman (1967) 'The effects of hearing one's own voice on sleep mentation', *Journal of Nervous and Mental Disease*, 144, p. 2–13.

23. D. Foulkes, T. Pivik, H. S. Steadman, P. S. Spear and J. D. Symonds (1967) 'Dreams of the male child: the EEG study', *Journal of Abnormal Psychology*, 72, pp. 457–67.

24. C. Winget, M. Kramer and R. Whitman (1970) 'The relationship of socio-economic status and race to dream content', *Psychophysiology*, 7, pp. 325–6.

25. C. B. Brenneis (1970) 'Male and female ego modalities in manifest dream content', *Journal of Abnormal Psychology*, 76, pp. 434–42.

26. C. S. Hall and R. L. Van de Castle (1965) 'An empirical investigation of the castration complex in dreams', *Journal of Personality*, 33, pp. 20–9.

27. L. Breger *et al.* (1971) *op. cit.*

28. S. Fisher and R. P. Greenberg (1977) *op. cit.*

29. C. S. Hall and R. L. Van de Castle (1966) *The Content Analysis of Dreams*, New York, Appleton, Century-Crofts.

30. W. Reis (1951) 'A comparison of the interpretation of dream series with and without free association', unpublished doctoral dissertation; Western Reserve University, cited by S. Fisher and R. P. Greenberg (1977), *op. cit.*

31. For example, L. Minturn (1965) 'A cross-cultural linguistic analysis of Freudian symbols', *Ethnology*, 4, pp. 336–42.

32. C. Fisher, J. Gross and J. Zuch (1965) 'Cycle of penile erection synchronous with dreaming (REM) sleep', *Archives of General Psychiatry*, 12, pp. 29–45.

33. C. Fisher (1965) 'Psychoanalytic implications of recent research on sleep and dreaming', *Journal of the American Psychoanalytic Association*, 13, pp. 197–303.

34. See W. C. Dement (1960) 'The effect of dream deprivation', *Science*, 131, pp. 1705–7.

35. R. D. Cartwright, L. J. Monroe and C. Palmer (1967) 'Individual differences in response to REM deprivation', *Archives of General Psychiatry*, 16, pp. 297–303.

36. F. Hoedemaker, A. Kales, A. Jacobson and E. Lichtenstein (1963) 'Dream

deprivation: an experimental re-appraisal'; cited in S. Fisher and R. Greenberg (1977) *op. cit.*

37. R. Greenberg, C. Pearlman, R. Fingar, J. Kantrowitz and S. Kawliche (1970) 'The effects of dream deprivation: implications for a theory of the psychological function of dreaming', *British Journal of Medical Psychology*, 43, pp. 1–11.

38. A. Gesell and F. L. Ilg (1942) *Infant and Child in the Culture of Today*, London, Hamish Hamilton.

39. For example, see L. J. Yarrow (1954) 'The relationship between nutritive sucking experiences in infancy and non-nutritive sucking in childhood', *Journal of Genetic Psychology*, 84, pp. 149–62.

40. H. L. Duthie and F. W. Gairns (1960) 'Sensory nerve-endings and sensations in the anal region of man', *British Journal of Surgery*, 47, pp. 585–9.

41. B. A. Farrell (1981) *op. cit.*

42. The Dynamic Personality Inventory, for example, constructed by T. G. Grygier (1961) specifically for measuring psychoanalytically defined attributes is frequently used but its validity is open to considerable question.

43. V. Lerner (1961) 'Auditory and visual thresholds for the perception of words of anal connotation: an evaluation of the sublimation hypothesis on philatelists'; unpublished doctoral dissertation, cited by S. Fisher and R. P. Greenberg (1977) *op. cit.*

44. G. C. Rosenwald (1972) 'Effectiveness of defenses against anal impulse arousal', *Journal of Consulting and Clinical Psychology*, 39, pp. 292–8.

45. P. Kline (1981) *op. cit.*

46. S. Fisher and R. P. Greenberg (1977) *op. cit.*

47. K. Abraham (1927) 'The influence of oral erotism on character formation'. In *Selected Papers*, London, Hogarth Press, pp. 383–406.

48. E. K. Beller (1957) 'Dependency and autonomous achievement striving related to orality and anality in early childhood', *Child Development*, 28, pp. 287–315.

49. C. D. Noblin (1962) 'Experimental analysis of psychoanalytic character types through the operant conditioning of verbal response', *American Psychologist*, 17, p. 306; E. O. Timmons and C. D. Noblin (1963) 'The differential performance of orals and anals in a verbal conditioning paradigm', *Journal of Consulting Psychology*, 27, pp. 383–6.

50. L. C. Robbins (1963) 'The accuracy of parental recall of aspects of child development and of child-rearing practices, *Journal of Abnormal and Social Psychology*, 66, pp. 262–70.

51. J. W. Whiting and I. L. Child (1953) *Child Training and Personality*, New Haven, Yale University Press.

52. P. Kline (1981) *op. cit.*

53. S. M. Friedman (1952) 'An empirical study of the castration and Oedipus complexes', *Genetic Psychology Monographs*, 46, pp. 61–130.

54. See, for example, C. S. Hall (1963) 'Strangers in dreams; an empirical confirmation of the Oedipus complex', *Journal of Personality*, 31, pp. 336–45.

55. C. S. Hall and R. L. Van de Castle (1965) *op. cit.*

56. S. M. Friedman (1952) *op. cit.*

57. I. Sarnoff and S. M. Corwin (1959) 'Castration anxiety and the fear of death', *Journal of Personality*, 27, pp. 374–85.
58. A. I. Rabin (1958) 'Some psychosexual differences between Kibbutz and non-Kibbutz Israeli boys', *Journal of Projective Techniques*, 22, pp. 328–32.
59. W. N. Stephens (1962) *The Oedipus Complex Hypothesis: Cross-cultural Evidence*, New York, Free Press.
60. B. A. Farrell (1981) *op. cit.*
61. S. Fisher and R. P. Greenberg (1977) *op. cit.*, pp. 221–2.
62. G. B. Johnson (1966) 'Penis envy or pencil needing?' *Psychological Reports*, 19, p. 758.
63. H. G. Harlow (1958) 'The nature of love', *American Psychologist*, vol. 13, pp. 673–85.
64. J. Bowlby (1952) *Maternal Care and Mental Health*, WHO Monograph, 2nd edition.
65. See, for instance, M. Rutter (1981) *Maternal Deprivation Reassessed*, Harmondsworth, Penguin Books; R. W. Clark and A. D. Clarke (1976) (eds.) *Early Experience: Myth and Evidence*, London, Open Books.
66. F. R. Wilkinson and D. W. Carghill (1955) 'Repression elicited by story material based on the Oedipus complex', *Journal of Social Psychology*, 42, pp. 209–14.
67. G. Levinger and J. Clark (1961) 'Emotional factors in the forgetting of word associations', *Journal of Abnormal and Social Psychology*, 62, pp. 95–105.
68. For example, R. S. Lazarus and R. A. McCleary (1951) 'Autonomic discrimination without awareness: a study of subception', *Psychological Review*, 58, pp. 113–22; N. F. Dixon and M. Haider (1961) 'Changes in the visual threshold as a function of subception', *Quarterly Journal of Experimental Psychology*, 13, pp. 229–35.
69. G. S. Blum (1955) 'Perceptual defense revisited', *Journal of Abnormal and Social Psychology*, 51, pp. 24–9.
70. J. Dollard, L. W. Doob, N. E. Miller, O. J. Mowrer and R. R. Sears (1939) *Frustration and Aggression*, New Haven, Yale University Press.
71. N. E. Miller and R. Bugelski (1948) 'Minor studies of aggression II: the influence of frustrations imposed by the in-group on attitudes expressed towards out-groups', *Journal of Psychology*, 25, pp. 437–42.
72. S. Freud (1911) *Psychoanalytic Notes on an Autobiographical Account of a Case of Paranoia*, Standard Edition, vol. XII.
73. H. S. Zamansky (1958) 'An investigation of the psychoanalytic theory of paranoid delusions', *Journal of Personality*, 26, pp. 410–25.
74. K. M. Colby (1963) 'Computer simulation of a neurotic process', in S. Tomkins and S. Messick (eds.) *Computer Simulation of Personality: Frontiers of Psychological Theory*, New York, Wiley.
75. S. Freud (1895) *Project for a Scientific Psychology*, Standard Edition, vol. I, p. 285.
76. See, for example, M. Kanzer (1973) 'Two prevalent misconceptions about Freud's project (1895)', *Annual of Psychoanalysis*, vol. 1, New York, Quadrangle, pp. 88–103.
77. K. Pribram and M. Gill (1976) *Freud's Project Reassessed*, London, Hutchinson.

78. R. W. Sperry (1969) 'A modified concept of consciousness', *Psychological Review*, 76, pp. 532–636.
79. J. C. Eccles (1970) *Facing Reality*, New York, Springer-Verlag.
80. K. Pribram and M. Gill (1976) *op. cit.*, p. 21.
81. *ibid.*, p. 168.
82. S. Freud (1933) *New Introductory Lectures in Psychoanalysis*, Standard Edition, vol. XXII, p. 152.
83. B. Brody (1970) 'Freud's case-load', *Psychotherapy: Theory, Research and Practice*, 7, pp. 8–12.
84. S. Fisher and R. P. Greenberg (1977) *op. cit.*
85. See, for example, C. P. Oberndorf, P. Greenacre and L. Kubie (1949) 'Symposium on the evaluation of therapeutic results'. *Yearbook of Psychoanalysis*, 5, pp. 9–34.
86. C. B. Truax and R. R. Carkhuff (1967) *Toward Effective Counselling and Psychotherapy*, Chicago, Aldine.
87. H. J. Eysenck (1952) 'The effects of psychotherapy: an evaluation', *Journal of Consulting Psychology*, 16, pp. 319–24.
88. See, for example, S. Rosenzweig (1954) 'A transvaluation of psychotherapy: a reply to Hans Eysenck', *Journal of Abnormal and Social Psychology*, 49, pp. 298–304; D. J. Kiesler (1966) 'Some myths of psychotherapy research and the search for a paradigm', *Psychological Bulletin*, 65, pp. 110–136.
89. C. Landis (1937) 'Statistical evaluation of psychotherapeutic methods', in L. E. Hinsie (ed.) *Concepts and Problems of Psychotherapy*, New York, Columbia University Press.
90. P. G. Denker (1947) 'Results of treatment of psychoneuroses by the general practitioner: a follow-up study of 500 patients', *Archives of Neurology and Psychiatry*, 57, pp. 504–5.
91. S. Rosenzweig (1954) *op. cit.*
92. For example, A. E. Bergin (1971) 'The evaluation of therapeutic outcomes'. In A. E. Bergin and S. L. Garfield (eds.) *Handbook of Psychotherapy and Behaviour Change*, New York, Wiley, pp. 217–70.
93. P. Kline (1981) *op. cit.*, p. 398.
94. For example, H. Schjelderup (1955) 'Lasting effects of psychoanalytic treatment', *Psychiatry*, 18, pp. 103–33; S. Z. Orgel (1958) 'Effect of psychoanalysis on the course of peptic ulcer', *Psychosomatic Medicine*, 20, pp. 117–23.
95. R. D. Cartwright (1966) 'A comparison of the response to psychoanalytic and client-centred psychotherapy', New York, Appleton-Century-Crofts.
96. L. Bellak (1958) 'Studying the psychoanalytic process by the method of short-range prediction and judgement', *British Journal of Medical Psychology*, 31, pp. 249–52.
97. D. Bannister (1980) 'The nonsense of effectiveness', *New Forum* (Journal of the Psychology and Psychotherapy Association), August.
98. S. Freud (1933) *op cit.*, pp. 156–7.
99. B. A. Farrell (1981) *op. cit.*
100. A. MacIntyre (1965) 'The psychoanalysts', *Encounter*, vol. 25, no. 5, pp. 38–43.

101. K. R. Popper (1955) 'Philosophy of science: a personal report', in C. A. Mace (ed.) *British philosophy in Mid-Century*, London, Allen and Unwin.
102. H. J. Eysenck and G. D. Wilson (1973) *The Experimental Study of Freudian Theories*, London, Methuen.
103. B. A. Farrell (1981) *op. cit.*
104. *ibid.*, p. 44.

Chapter 11 – The Significance of Meaning

1. K. Hart (1981) 'Memories of a survivor against all odds', *Company Magazine*, August.
2. S. Freud (1895) *Project for a Scientific Psychology*, Standard Edition, vol. I, p. 309.
3. J. Lacan (1979) *The Four Fundamental Concepts of Psychoanalysis*, trans. by A. Sheridan, Harmondsworth, Penguin.
4. S. Freud (1900) *The Interpretation of Dreams*, Standard Edition, vol. IV, pp. 277–78.
5. R. I. Munroe (1955) *Schools of Psychoanalytic Thought*, New York, Holt, Rinehart and Winston, p. 272.
6. J. Habermas (1972) *Knowledge and Human Interests*, trans. by J. J. Shapiro, London, Heinemann, p. 214.
7. Ethnography would also lay claim to incorporate methodological self-reflection.
8. B. A. Farrell (1981) *The Standing of Psychoanalysis*, Oxford, Oxford University Press, p. 212.
9. S. Freud (1917) *Introductory Lectures on Psychoanalysis*, Standard Edition, vol. XVI, p. 244.
10. F. Cioffi (1970) 'Freud and the idea of a pseudo-science', in M. R. Borger and F. Cioffi (eds) *Explanation in the Behavioural Sciences*, Cambridge, Cambridge University Press.
11. S. Freud (1926) *The Question of Lay Analysis*, Standard Edition, vol. XX, p. 219.
12. S. Freud (1920) *Beyond the Pleasure Principle*, Standard Edition, vol. XVIII, p. 24.
13. *ibid.*, p. 64.
14. *ibid.*, p. 38.
15. S. Freud (1925) *An Autobiographical Study*, Standard Edition, vol. XX, p. 70.
16. Freud, quoted by L. Binswanger (1957) *Sigmund Freud: Reminiscences of a Friendship*, New York and London, Grune and Stratton.
17. A. MacIntyre (1965) 'The psychoanalysts', *Encounter*, vol. 25, no. 5, pp. 38–43.
18. *ibid.*, p. 43.
19. P. Rieff (1965) *Freud: The Mind of the Moralist*, London, Methuen.
20. *ibid.*, pp. 26–27.

Chapter 12 – A Personal Creation

1. E. H. Erikson (1968) *Identity: Youth and Crisis*, London, Faber, p. 43.
2. S. Freud (1937) 'A disturbance of memory on the Acropolis', in Standard Edition, vol. XXII, pp. 237–52.
3. E. Jones (1953–7) *The Life and Work of Sigmund Freud*, London, Hogarth Press. Abridged by L. Trilling and S. Marcus (1964), Harmondsworth, Penguin.
4. S. Freud (1917) 'A Childhood Recollection', from *Dichtung und Wahrheit*, Standard Edition, vol. XVII, p. 156.
5. S. Freud (1925) *An Autobiographical Study*, Standard Edition, vol. XX.
6. F. J. Sulloway (1979) *Freud, Biologist of the Mind*, London, Burnett Books.
7. P. Roazen (1970) *Brother Animal: the Story of Freud and Tausk*, London, Allen Lane.
8. O. Gillie and P. Swales (1982) 'The secret love life of Sigmund Freud', *Sunday Times*, January. But see A. C. Elms (1982) 'Freud and Minna', *Psychology Today*, December, pp. 40–46, for criticism of their analysis.
9. R. D. Stolorow and G. E. Atwood (1979) *Faces in a Cloud: Subjectivity in Personality Theory*, New York, Aronson.
10. *ibid.*, p. 48.
11. S. Freud (1899) in *The Origins of Psychoanalysis: Letters to Wilhelm Fliess, Drafts and Notes, (1887–1902)*, edited by M. Bonaparte, A. Freud and E. Kris (1954) London, Imago, p. 262.
12. *ibid.*
13. *ibid.*, p. 264.
14. S. Freud (1901) *The Psychopathology of Everyday Life*, trans. by A. Tyson, Pelican Freud Library, vol. 5, Harmondsworth, Penguin.
15. S. Freud (1900) *The Interpretation of Dreams*, Standard Edition, vol. V, p. 583.
16. S. Freud (1933) *New Introductory Lectures in Psychoanalysis*, Standard Edition, vol. XXII, p. 133.
17. Freud, quoted by E. Jones (1953), *The Life and Work of Sigmund Freud*, London, Hogarth Press. Abridged by L. Trilling and S. Marcus (1964), Harmondsworth, Penguin, p. 102.
18. *ibid.*, p. 29.
19. S. Tomkins (1963) *Affect, Imagery, Consciousness, vol. II: The Negative Affects.*
20. S. Freud (1933) *op. cit.*
21. *ibid.*, pp. 121–2.
22. *ibid.*, p. 123.
23. S. Freud (1925) 'Some psychical consequences of the anatomical distinction between the sexes', Standard Edition, vol. XIX, pp. 257–8.
24. R. D. Stolorow and G. E. Atwood (1979) *op. cit.*, p. 67.

Chapter 13 – Moral Implications and Social Impact

1. E. Fromm (1960) *Fear of Freedom*, London, Routledge and Kegan Paul, p. 10.
2. P. Rieff (1965) *Freud: The Mind of the Moralist*, London, Methuen.

3. S. Freud (1913) *Totem and Taboo*, Standard Edition, vol. XIII.
4. S. Freud (1927) *The Future of an Illusion*, Standard Edition, vol. XXII.
5. S. Freud (1930) *Civilization and its Discontents*, Standard Edition, vol. XXI.
6. R. W. Clark (1980) *Freud: The Man and the Cause*, New York, Random House, p. 355.
7. S. Freud (1930) *op. cit.*, p. 134.
8. S. Freud (1926) *The Question of Lay Analysis*, Standard Edition, vol. XX.
9. Passage interpolated into Freud's text. See S. Freud (1938) *The Basic Writings of Sigmund Freud*, trans. by A. A. Brill, New York, Random House, p. 57.
10. Otto Rank, quoted in T. Szasz (1977) *Karl Kraus and the Soul-Doctors*, London, Routledge and Kegan Paul, p. 38.
11. E. H. Erikson (1950) *Childhood and Society*, New York, Norton. Reprinted in paperback (1977) by Triad/Paladin, p. 238.
12. S. Freud (1930) *op. cit.*, p. 64.

Chapter 14 – Explorations in Awareness

1. E. H. Erikson (1968) *Identity: Youth and Crisis*, London, Faber, p. 43.
2. See R. Stevens (1976) *Understanding Social Behaviour and Experience*, Social Psychology, Block 1, Milton Keynes, The Open University Press.
3. E. H. Erikson (1950) *Childhood and Society*, New York, Norton. Reprinted in paperback (1977) by Triad/Paladin, p. 364.
4. E. H. Erikson (1975) *Life History and the Historical Moment*, New York, Norton, p. 39.

INDEX

Bold numbers indicate a major reference to a person or concept. Italicized numbers denote an entry in *References and Notes*.